MW01026969

BEYOND DEATH

BROTHERS FOREVER

AN UNEXPECTED JOURNEY BEYOND DEATH

JOSEPH GALLENBERGER, PH.D.

HAMPTON ROADS
PUBLISHING COMPANY, INC.

Copyright © 1996
by Joseph Mark Gallenberger, Ph.D.

All rights reserved, including the right to reproduce this
work in any form whatsoever, without permission
in writing from the publisher, except for brief passages
in connection with a review.

Cover design by Marjoram Productions
Cover photo by Jon Friedman

For information write:

Hampton Roads Publishing Company, Inc.
134 Burgess Lane
Charlottesville, VA 22902

Or call: (804) 296-2772
FAX: (804) 296-5096
e-mail: hrpc@mail.hamptonroadspub.com
Web site: http://www.hamptonroadspub.com

If you are unable to order this book from your local
bookseller, you may order directly from the publisher.
Quantity discounts for organizations are available.
Call 1-800-766-8009, toll-free.

ISBN 1-57174-045-7

10 9 8 7 6 5 4 3 2 1

Printed on acid-free paper in the United States of America

In memory of my brother,

Peter Joseph Gallenberger

We can be shrouded by grief's dark cocoon
and re-emerge with great lightness
of heart and richness of spirit.
This is surely a sign that we are magical creatures!

CONTENTS

Acknowledgments

I thank my family and friends who held me in a circle of love through the loss of my brother. I extend deep appreciation to my wife Charleene and to my daughter Sarah Beth, for cheerfully supporting me with my writing in many essential ways.

Preface

All humans experience loss. That is unavoidable fact. When someone we love dies, we are driven to wonder and worry whether that loved one is now at peace. Near-death experiences hint at what may go on during the process of dying and shortly thereafter but do not address what happens after that. Traditional Christianity claims only that the dead exist in a constant unchanging state of heaven or hell.

Now there are new sources of information about what we experience after physical death. These sources suggest a rich, varied, and changing life of the spirit, with the possibility of at least some communication between those living in the physical and those who have died. The science and psychology of these links are beginning to be explored. This book provides a new outlook on life and death, clearly identifying what is currently known and what is an educated guess in this field of inquiry.

This true story speaks also about a type of love seldom explored. It probes the rich interweaving of a lifetime of relating as brothers—at times close, at times distant, exchanging roles of giver and receiver, but ever deepening into a love that pierces through the veil of death.

In addition, the book is about suicide and conquering the grief that follows such an action. More than ten million of us have survived the suicide of someone close to us. Survivors of suicide feel the shock, denial, helplessness, and sadness of all sudden deaths but also statistically experience more depression, fear of aloneness, and relationship problems. When someone close to us chooses death, that person renounces our power to help. This renunciation tempts the survivor to feel a persistent worthlessness and guilt. Many survivors are silent about their pain. Most need to release their pain by talking it out with someone who will listen and will not judge.

I want to tell you the story of the mysteries of life and death that my brother Peter and I are sharing. I hope my book helps you avoid harsh judgment of yourself or another if you are ever affected by suicide and encourages you to explore your concerns about what you or a loved one might experience after death—thereby increasing the love and peace of us all.

1 ∞ DEPARTURE

My first memories of Pete were formed just after we moved to a Jersey suburb. During their house hunting, my folks feared that they would not find a decent place to raise their family of seven. Rural Midwest Catholic values strained to fit this new environment. And my parent's modest savings meant little so close to that pounding heart of commerce, New York City. They felt fortunate to find a large old colonial in bad repair in a stable neighborhood with maples and oaks overhanging the streets. I was five years old and Pete was thirteen when we moved in.

Our resettlement omens were not good. We arrived in the fall of 1954 just hours before the full force of Hurricane Carol came roaring through. I peered into the black cavern of the huge Mayflower van, eye-level to the floor of the truck, anxiously waiting for my bicycle to resurrect itself, as the wind began to howl. Strong men were struggling, tacking left and right toward the front door with the mattresses they were carrying. Once we were inside with our possessions, the power went off and we spent the first day and night listening to oaks crack and crash around our new neighborhood. Pete comforted me while my folks set up a base camp within the house.

Over the years, we worked hard to put the charm back into that old house. I can still remember that first winter, working in yeasty humidity, steaming off a mile of worn, dark maroon damask wallpaper, my knuckles scraping the rough plaster underneath. It felt five-year-old great to peel off a really long piece, intact, from ten-foot-high walls. As fresh mint-greens, whites, and creams transformed the walls, and light apricot carpeting went down, we knew we would win the struggle.

The woozy smell of wood-stripper and its bite on the skin accompanied restoration of the stairs and banister. As the weather warmed a bit, we attacked the outside. The fragrances of leaf mold, fifty years ancient, and of fresh-cut wood danced together deep into my lungs as we trimmed back towering rhododendrons that hid the leaded windows in front of the house.

Pete and I worked side by side around this house. He showed me how to make a game out of picking up vast quantities of shattered glass that rose shimmering to the surface each spring in the back yard. By the time I was ten, those shards had become as rare as treasure. Pete showed me how to sow seed evenly and care for the fragile lawn until it thrived. Our house finally became a beautiful home. We had learned the value of work and enjoyed its results.

My parents had four boys, each four years apart, followed by a girl two years later. Pete was the second child and I the last boy. All of us were born in the snowy season, which in Wisconsin lasts half the year. We moved to the East Coast when my dad started climbing his corporate ladder. Both my parents were very busy during that time, so Pete took up the slack and often served as my mother, father, friend, and mentor. In the flow of time, I have had the privilege of returning each of these blessings to him.

Eight years older, he volunteered to diaper me as an infant, play with me when I was a toddler, and counsel me on playground tactics as I started school. I don't remember him wasting time or expecting someone else to come up with his entertainment. He enjoyed competition and abhorred poor sportsmanship. I never saw him angry at our parents. He seemed always to be performing "up to specs." Perhaps he missed part of his own childhood—the chance to be at times weak, scared, petulant, or selfish. To me, he has been a magical interplay of dark and light, and always the adult.

During my childhood and his adolescence, Pete set an example of excellent appearance: dressing cool, building his body to perfection, and keeping his car gleaming. He would work summers, sunup to sundown, cutting lawns. Then he would come home, lift weights, shower, dress, and go out in his shiny chariot. He had many different automobiles as a teenager, mostly convertibles—all fast ones with perfect paint, paid for with his own money. These cars granted freedom, embodied power, and promised adventure—things he cherished at a soul level then and throughout his life.

The schools in our town had a reputation for excellence. Yet Pete cared little about school. When I was a kid, I had the sense that the classroom was a prison for him, as it was for me. His bright intellect was creative, playful, and Socratic. And he liked to see immediate results from his actions. He was a doer, and any knowledge had to pass the test of practicality. He sought fairness for everyone. Later, Pete confessed that he had found school agonizingly slow, dulling, senseless, and arbitrary in its application of rules. He may have been what is now called attention-deficit disordered: very restless when information is coming in too slowly and anxious when stimulation is coming in too fast.

What I most admired about Pete as I was growing up and what I still treasure is that he treated all life forms (human, animal, or plant) with an intelligent, quiet kindness and respect. And he did so in a very manly way. Adults, peers, and children all responded to him with a great attraction. So he set an example which seemed to me both worthy and reachable. If I could follow it, I felt guaranteed to become a good man, well-liked and successful. Of all my hand-me-downs, his were the best. Yet they also contained a dangerous shadow.

As he disappeared into college, his clothing remained as a tangible echo. His muscle shirts were stretched large at the biceps; I worked hard to have them fit my younger arms tightly. After Pete went away, I took over some of his chores, but each in our family missed his spark of bright, loving power.

Many years later, I learned that he had not wanted to go to college. He yearned instead to open a pool parlor and wanted my folks to use his college money to back him. He was eager to get on with life, to be where the action was and build something new and vibrant. But my folks stood firm. My Dad had been the first in his family to complete college. That education had taken him from farming to the vice-presidency of a printing company, launching him into the larger world. He was committed to providing a similar opportunity to each of his five children.

Pete, knuckling under to my folks' wisdom or fear, tried my Dad's alma mater, Lawrence College, in Wisconsin. Freshmen had to live on campus and could have no car. Pete suffered through a first year's snows, feeling isolated and restricted. He left college in the spring.

He escaped by joining the Army, presenting his enlistment as a surprise and expecting everyone to be happy for him. But Vietnam was heating up, and we worried that he would be killed. My folks also felt that he was wasting his talents. I think Peter felt that, if he could not follow my folks' wishes for him, he should pay his own way to follow his own dream.

I can remember a series of phone calls during this time, after which my folks seemed weakened, muted, and sad. They were torn between a deep commitment to give each of their children full freedom and a dread that Pete was digging his hole deeper. I know, however, that there was no "You are not making us proud" pressure. Rather, love and support were extended along with unheeded advice.

I was amazed at Pete's rebellion—his refusal to continue college. This stand did not fit my image of him. Our shining star further transformed into the black sheep when he announced that he was dropping the Church and planning to marry a non-Catholic. I watched this hushed family drama with great interest, sensing that someday I too might need to rebel. It was encouraging to see love hold but frightening to see the pain that this revolt caused. I attempted to ease family pain by trying to become as perfect as he used to be.

On a cloudy, quiet summer's day, two long years after he left us, Pete glided back home in a red Corvair convertible that purred perfectly at idle. He got out of the car and stood tall in dress uniform. He sported medals for marksmanship and a fianceé at his side. That fall their wedding took place in swirling gold leaves and bright sunshine. Then he disappeared again. He finished his tour working in Army intelligence.

Pete found me later, when I needed rescue. I was being kicked out of a monastery school at fifteen years of age—angry, lonely, frightened, and disillusioned. The headmasters felt that I wasn't monk material, being too challenging of authority. They were probably right. But from the time of fifth grade I had fiercely wanted to become a priest. I had a deep love of God and wanted to help people. At the moment my dream failed, I could conceive of no other life.

Pete came, got me, and took me to his world. It was a tiny, cinder block house in Utica, New York. The yard looked worn in late winter. The surrounding snow was dirty gray. But his house sparkled white. He seemed very pleased to see me. Pete was twenty-three years old at that time.

He had two German Shepherds, one pure white and one dark, that he had trained with a whisper. They guarded his two-year-old son silently, like library lions. Pete's wife and son were clearly devoted to him. My first night there, in the glow and the smell of the kerosine heater in his basement guest room, I felt safe for the first time in two seasons and slept peacefully. Before bed, he had joked that now the family had two black sheep. I was comforted that he had paved the way. If I was not a failure in his eyes, perhaps I could really face myself and go on.

I followed him around for a few days, as he made his way between two jobs: cigarette-machine route salesman and night clerk at a motel. He worked hard, and I was impressed with the caring and intelligence he applied to his work. Later, still in Utica, he would work three eight-hour-a-day jobs at the same time, after a try at establishing his own business had failed. He survived on almost no sleep for months as he strived to get back on sound financial footing. He bravely presented this period as an experiment in micro-sleep, where he learned to catch a moment of slumber every time he blinked his eyes.

Despite the pressure Pete was under as I came out of the

seminary, he was eager to help me and shared all that he had. I wanted to try snowmobiling. He took me out, even though it was a windy twenty-below zero, and the locks were frozen on his car. Laughing together, we decided to end the adventure before we actually rode, when the reality of the cold sunk into our flesh. I felt close to him and very loved.

I stayed two weeks with Pete, and then it was time to go back to my parents. We stood by each other, bracing against the wind, at the small run-down train station, not saying much till we saw the engine's light. Then we exchanged smiles and a brief hug. When he put me on the train I was in much better shape than when he had picked me up.

Over the next twenty-five years we saw each other mostly during holidays when the whole family gathered. He seemed reserved during these visits—cordial but somehow uncomfortable. On the rare occasions when I visited with him privately, he would loosen up as we nestled under afghans at opposite ends of a sofa and share his deeper thoughts as we talked into the night. As I grew into adulthood, we bonded as brothers and friends. Still, he remained mostly a mystery.

After I married and moved down South, there were no private visits for many years. During family gatherings, I could sense his growing frustration over his own inability to capture the American Dream. Yet he was genuinely happy to hear of the blessings that others in our family were enjoying.

During these two decades, Pete's life didn't go well. Financial pressures were constant. It seemed that every job he tried resulted in failure. And he tried many occupations, usually in sales, sometimes in services—always hoping for the big score. When he sold cars, then motor homes, copiers, and real estate, he would be out of rhythm, hitting recessions and gas crunches at the wrong times. Sometimes people took advantage of his good nature. In other situations, he would lose confidence and sell himself short.

His marriage may have been impulsive; I am not sure. Over the years, the stress of finances and his deepening depression took a heavy toll on it, and the marriage ceased to bring him joy. His son was one bright source of love and hope. Yet even in that relationship there was tension.

The son's personality and interests were different from his father's in almost every way. For example, his son had no interest in cars, and still doesn't own one to this day. Pete did encourage his child to get an education, preferably in a trade that guaranteed a good living, such as plumbing. No doubt Pete felt his own unprepared path was a mistake. His son's path was to major in languages in college. Pete, despite subsistence-level income and his belief that language study was impractical, paid his son's way fully through college, including a Master's program. He did so by running up massive credit card debt, and eventually he was forced to declare bankruptcy.

Pete's pain and bitterness began to surface more strongly, despite his efforts to shield us from it. He attended fewer family functions, but we could count on seeing him at weddings and funerals and at Christmas time. We were a family of high achievers, executives, and professionals. All his siblings had earned graduate degrees. It was obviously hard for him to listen to our conversations of success, not so much from jealousy, as from his sense of isolation—that his life experience had little in common with ours due to what he felt were his own failings. He was slipping away.

I suspect that our family is genetically prone to depression. My own despondency during college got me into psychotherapy. After therapy, my despair was controlled but still surfaced with unwanted regularity until it waned in my late thirties. My depression occurred in the context of outward abundance and loving friendships. When I was depressed, joy was suffocated by a great, dark, soul-quaking heaviness. I can only wonder at what that weight must have felt like for Pete, lacking the support of material and relationship success.

When Pete was in his mid-thirties, a kid in a speeding Cadillac ran a stop sign and smashed into the driver's side of his car. Pete was severely injured. He sustained a crushed left arm (he was left-handed) and a broken left thigh. We now had something traumatic in common.

When I was twenty-one, I had broken my left thigh in a motorcycle wreck and had spent nearly a year in the hospital. I had rods drilled through my leg without anesthesia, was strung up in traction for four months, and then was confined to a body cast. Roaches crawled in and out of my cast in the inner-city hospital. The immobility was maddening for me, as I had always been active as a swimmer and a runner. I was panicky and tearful often during my recovery.

When I heard the news of Pete's accident, I vomited, knowing what was ahead of him. When I saw him in the hospital, he appeared shaken but stoic. He was gracious to his guests and glad to see me. Pete's recovery was slow and incomplete. Some of his handsomeness and physical strength were taken from him; and physical pain became his constant companion.

Pete re-entered my life when he divorced and moved to the Carolina coast, within six hours of my home in the mountains of North Carolina. The warm climate allowed much outdoors time. He had always loved the ocean and the sun, and now he tanned darkly.

My wife and I had purchased a ridge-top ranch with a 360-degree view of the Smoky Mountains and the Blue Ridge and eight acres of rolling land. We had refurbished it lovingly and had added daffodils, roses, and all manner of grapes, berries, and fruit trees, as well as a big vegetable garden. At the beginning we went overboard with the joy of country life and planted two acres of corn by hand. Needless to say, we had enough corn for years and the crows had an absolute feast. Our crows consider us their friends for life and appear immediately when we go outside even to get the mail, on the off chance that I'm ready to repeat the great corn experiment!

A few months after he moved to the coast, Pete came to visit with his new girlfriend. I couldn't believe the difference. He seemed relaxed, playful, and happy. He enjoyed the beauty of our mountain home, taking long walks through the woods hand-in-hand with his new life mate.

I remember one fabulous day when we flew a giant kite, chasing it to and fro in our pasture, then resting in the sun.

Later we devoured a sumptuous cookout, enjoyed the twilight then the stars, and finally moved inside. That evening, he surprised me by springing up to dance with his girlfriend to the Beach Boys music playing on the stereo. My wife and I joined in, laughing and dancing. There was no self-consciousness, only celebration of life.

I was hopeful that, with his girlfriend's obvious support and his better mood, Pete's luck would change. But his lack of work success continued through many new attempts at earning a living. The pattern was very puzzling. He was brilliant, hardworking, honest, personable, and fair. He was experienced in real estate, construction, and many different types of sales. The only drawbacks I could see were his slightly crippled left hand and leg and his lack of a college degree.

During job interviews, he tried to hide his growing insecurity. For the few days before an interview, you could see him building up his cheerfulness and confidence, making an effort to turn his nervousness into energy and excitement. After practicing for the session, he dressed perfectly, shoes shined to a military gleam, and went to slay the dragon. But within himself, Pete was developing a theory that he was somehow cursed and that any project he might be part of would also be cursed. Although he was a great poker player and could bluff with the best, his theory may have been telegraphed unconsciously to prospective employers, causing them to shun him.

After a few years, he began to realize that the woman with whom he was living was becoming tired of his work failures and his despair. She couldn't stand to see the man she loved, who seemed a better man than any other she had met, in so much constant pain. They separated. He accepted my offer to come to live in my town.

We set up an apartment for him in the upstairs of the old home where I had my psychology practice. It was humble surroundings, but he seemed genuinely glad to stay there. He put his bed, refrigerator, microwave, and a long table in one room. Dishes were washed in the bathroom sink. In the other room, he built shelves out of cinder block and scrap wood to hold his books. He was an avid reader. A sofa, TV, and his treasured miniature classic car collection completed the decor.

He kept the place immaculate and planted many flowers around the grounds. I would arrive at work to find him bent over and shirtless, glistening in the early southern sun, tending the plants. He would stiffly straighten with a smile. Filled with affection for him, I would try to keep my eyes from lingering too long on the scars which deformed his arm.

I was delighted and honored. I was having a chance to spend extended time with my older brother for whom I had the deepest respect. I went upstairs to his apartment whenever I had a break in work. He would greet me with his gentle smile and fresh orange juice, pretzels, or pizza, depending upon the hour. We would sharpen our intellects together, then talk from the heart. His thinking was deep and probing, and his interests ranged widely.

One of our mutual interests was the work of Robert Monroe. We both had read *Journeys Out of the Body*.[1] Mr. Monroe was a businessman who had experiences in which he felt his consciousness float away from his body. He traveled freely in this nonphysical state. The book excited us because Pete and I had both enjoyed such experiences in childhood. Mine often began when I would awaken enough within a dream to be conscious of what was going on.

I would find myself, filled with excitement, rocketing down a big hill on my bike. Slowly and silently, the handlebars would separate and begin to rise, with me holding on, as the bike dropped beneath on its path downhill. At that point I would begin to have control within the dream. I'd let go of the handlebars and feel as if I were flying low over the treetops with great freedom and joy. I could cruise the town's streets, just above the telephone wires, and land at friends' houses or favorite places in the woods. Then I would fly home, feeling a jarring sensation as I re-entered my body on the bed. For days after one of these experiences, I would be filled with energy and a sense of well-being.

Many people report having some type of out-of-body experience (OBE) spontaneously a few times in their lives, particularly as children. Mr. Monroe had them nightly as an adult and had learned to induce and control them at will. Research of the OBE phenomenon has since been undertaken by others, including Keith Haray, Ph.D., and Pamela Weintraub at Duke University and the Institute for Advanced Psychology in Los Angeles.

When Pete came to live with me, he brought Monroe's sequel, *Far Journeys*.[2] It renewed my interest in this area, which had been quiescent since graduate school.

I had experienced a vivid OBE when I was twenty-one during my motorcycle accident. When the car hit me, I felt enormous pain that awed me with its totality. It had a terrible beauty, much like that of an atomic blast. It overwhelmed the senses and entranced my consciousness. This moment of pain was followed by complete surprise at finding myself floating peacefully and completely pain-free, about ten feet above my body. I looked down with complete unconcern at my body in spasms in the street and the motorcycle strewn nearby. Looking back in the direction from which I had been traveling, I could see three lanes of traffic fast approaching. I found it an interesting show and was detached from what would happen when the traffic arrived. My perception of the physical world was crystal clear; my thought patterns were fully cogent and logical. There was no doubt that this was real and not just some biochemically induced hallucination after trauma.

Then I felt an angelically light presence and its will that I return to my body. I resisted, telepathically argued, and lost. As I re-entered my body, the pain was no longer beautiful; rather, it was agony tainted with severe worry about how damaged I was and the hurt that was sure to follow. Then I blacked out and continued to go in and out of consciousness as the paramedics did their caring work and I was transported to the hospital. I remember screaming some, too.

During my hospital stay and for a few years after that, I attempted to consciously induce OBEs with some limited success. I then dropped my experiments in the fullness of marriage and parenting. OBEs have much in common with near-death experiences. Both are often transformative and leave the person knowing—not just believing—that there will be survival after the death of the physical body.

While he lived with us, Pete challenged me to take carefully considered risks in business. For me, money had always been tied to hours of effort—throwing papers, cutting lawns, painting houses, and, later, working as a psychotherapist. He had a different perspective. As a salesman, he could put in countless hours with no pay-back, and at other times be at the right place or take the right gamble and make money quickly and easily.

Although Pete encouraged me to reach for my dreams and take risks, my witnessing his life situation paradoxically made me more fearful in some ways. I did take greater risks in terms of trying new things and risking small amounts of money, but I became more cautious of anything that could leave me jobless.

In many aspects of life, Pete was my mentor during this period. He taught me billiards. Playing pool, I entered into a space with him where competition was light and playful and both of us celebrated a good shot regardless of who made it. I'd leave the pool hall feeling centered and peaceful. He taught me how to enjoy the simplest things of life with more patience and gracefulness. He celebrated my gardening successes and complimented me on anything that I did well. He reminded me of my blessings and confronted me whenever I was being less than honest with myself or was blocked by fear. Yet, the most precious offering he gave me during this time was to let me help him.

So, Pete's living with me was a great gift. I had looked forward to getting to know my brother and ended up in deep friendship with him, finding myself talking more frankly about some things with him than I ever had with anyone else. It felt reassuring and connected just to be with him. Much was discussed and re-experienced about our childhoods—both the commonalities and the differences. Vietnam and the peace movement had taken place between us, and the culture had changed dramatically during the eight years that separated our travels through adolescence and into adulthood.

When he first came to live with me, I don't think he had much regard for clinical psychology as a profession, but he did respect the effort it had taken me to get there. With his own feeling about school, he admired me for sticking it out through four years of college then five years of graduate school, studying subjects such as human personality, abnormal psychology, neurophysiology, research design, and psychotherapy. During this time I produced a thesis and a dissertation on child abuse, and then I pursued a year of internship and two more of apprenticeship, before being able to practice independently. The eight years of post-college work always included time with a variety of patients in settings including prisons, mental retardation centers, mental health centers, college clinics, state hospitals, and private clinics. In these settings my feelings and knowledge about myself and my understanding about how life worked were constantly challenged by patients and supervisors alike.

Pete admired me for all my efforts and accomplishments, but his nature was to respect workers who produced something more tangible than I had to show for my work. He tried to understand my profession, however, and eventually appreciated the difficulties and satisfactions involved in the therapist role. This appreciation pleased me greatly, as his respect was important to me. His probing questions helped me sort out the wheat from the chaff delivered to me in all that training. He made me more aware of the importance of mundane practicalities in my patients' lives—how busyness, tiredness, financial strain, and responsibilities hampered one's quest for self-understanding and change.

Pete would particularly challenge any assumption he felt was too New Age or too liberal. He did not necessarily disagree with these philosophies but was on guard against any thinking that he considered illogical, "mushy headed," or not consistent with real-world experience. He would get almost angry when he felt people were using the word "love" too frivolously.

Despite all the richness I felt from his presence, he felt that he was mooching off me by paying no rent. Employment for middle-aged white males was drying up as the country headed toward its long late-'80s recession. His job search went no better in my area. And he was running out of money.

About two years after he had moved in with us, it became apparent how depressed and anxious he was. He seldom slept peacefully. Weekends during which he avoided all human contact were increasing. Pete refused therapy and medications despite much urging. He acknowledged their value for others but didn't see how they could help him. He felt that without a mate and without work, his life *was* truly depressing. And if anything made him content in the face of that, it could only do so at the expense of having him be out of touch with grim reality.

This stance was extremely frustrating for me, as I believed that psychotherapy and medications might help him. I repeatedly related to him all kinds of counseling success stories and went over the intricacies of how antidepressants work, trying to show him how they did not drug away selfhood, consciousness, or willpower. We replayed versions of the same conversation:

He would respond, "Well, how would talking to someone help me? What I need is a job."

I would propose, "Therapy could give you support, and let you vent your feelings instead of keeping them inside. It might even generate some new options you haven't thought of."

"I don't want to be humored or pitied. And all I do is think of options day and night. I have talked to you guys, friends, and job counselors about this over and over. Do you really think I could have missed anything that really would make a difference?"

"Why not try anyway? What have you got to lose?"

"How about the last of my self-respect and money!"

"Well then, how about trying medications? They may help you to sleep better and help with the pain. You are depressed. That impairs your concentration, creativity, and energy. You need to be at your best when you look for work. Medication can help with that."

"Of course I'm depressed. I would have to be crazy not to be depressed. I don't have the money to go to doctors and besides I just don't feel medication will help me get a job. Having that on my record might even keep me from getting a job and health insurance later."

If I pressed on, the final retort would be: "I tried therapy a long time ago. The shrink was well-meaning and skillful but it didn't help. Can we please just drop it?"

And so I would drop it with a final entreaty: "Please think about it."

One thing Pete did try was meditation. Through my seminary experience with centering prayer and, later, studies of an Egyptian system of focused concentration[3] and practice of Buddhist meditation, I could relax and enter a peaceful state where creativity was enhanced and options became apparent. I could then return energized and more calmly implement positive changes in my life. I felt this skill could help Pete. But regardless of the meditation system he tried, he would get restless instead of relaxed. I think that he was holding too much emotion to let his defenses down. He got most of his relief through long walks following the train tracks out of town and into the woods.

To appreciate Pete's view on life and on his chances for happiness, you need to understand the great importance he put on productivity and the string of frustrations he experienced in this area. From his point of view, his thirty-year work history was a string of disasters. Here are just a few examples. He gradually added one cigarette machine after another to his route in Utica. When he owned about twenty machines, he found them all smashed in one night. He had entered into Mafia territory without knowing it.

Desperate for quick money, he then purchased a race horse. The bottom fell out of a trailer as he was transporting it to its first race, killing the horse instantly. Large real estate deals he had worked on for years were finally consummated, only to have him cut out of the commissions by politicians who took bribes. He worked cleaning carpets—often on his knees, scraping gum off of barroom floors after closing time, until his damaged arm and leg could stand it no longer.

His last business before moving in with me was a used furniture business. It struggled through its first year, began to show promise, then collapsed when a fire forced him to move to a new location, undercapitalized.

It is hard to comprehend his efforts each time to start over in some new business, scraping up funds through menial jobs that barely allowed for food and rent. No employer would hire him at a salary above minimum wage; the only other offers he had were straight commission jobs that offered no benefits.

It was eerie how far and long his bad luck, if that was what it was, seemed to extend. When he came to live with me, the first job he tried involved selling computerized pay telephones. I bought his first one and installed it at a local golf course. It got struck by lightning the very first day, one day before the insurance on it took effect. He wouldn't have let me invest unless he was certain that I would enjoy a nice secure return, and now he felt guilty that I was out three thousand bucks. This weirdness was typical of what happened when Pete accepted help from someone.

Pete did nothing that I could see to directly sabotage his own efforts. He worked long and hard for thirty-five years, and his luck just continued to be amazingly bad. Picture keeping up your confidence in that situation and pulling deep from the gut to try once again. Now imagine doing it while burying most of the bitterness deep within yourself.

He felt that he could not get and keep a girlfriend until he had money. I doubt that he ever went Dutch on a date in his life. Perhaps his hopelessness was infectious; after a year of his living with me, I saw no option which he was willing to take that had a good chance of success. No option except that he find a job at a living wage.

As his job efforts in my small rural town reached a dead end, he began to mention suicide as his only way out. He was concerned that, if he lived much longer, his debts would finally wipe out all his life insurance, which was his only way to leave something for his son. He did not want to be a financial burden to anyone, particularly my folks, who were approaching eighty.

He did not qualify for disability, yet he was unable to find health insurance because of his injuries.

He resisted going back to college, feeling that his employ-ability would be very low when he graduated as a fifty-four-year-old white male with his physical limitations. He felt he couldn't risk other peoples' money on such a long shot. He looked into trade schools, but most programs involved manual strength and dexterity he no longer had, all cost money, and none guaranteed work.

Pete's thoughts of suicide ran to creative ways which would not be detectible, so that life insurance benefits would not be jeopardized. He considered hanging himself while standing on a block of dry ice in the woods so that it would look like someone else hanged him once the ice melted. I would counter that if he were far enough from people for this to work, he might never be found.

He then speculated that he could wait at a rest stop with a gun. When another car stopped, he could tie a string between the gun and the car bumper and run a short distance into the woods. As the car pulled away, the gun would fire. After the shot, the string would carry the weapon away and the string would wear out miles up the road, letting the gun tumble into the brush along the side of the road. It would look like murder, not suicide.

I took these dark fantasies seriously and yet understood that in the face of the intolerable current pain, he needed to have hope that there was an eventual way out of struggle. Most times he said these things in a way that allowed us to think he was just letting off steam. I would try to assure him of his value and help him generate some hope. Much of what they taught me in school—that suicidal thoughts were often anger turned inward; to help the person see past the current pain and realize that life continually changed; to encourage support systems and action to reduce stress and dissatisfaction—these were all shadowed by the knowledge that depression could be lethal.

The examples of suicide we were given in school were too easy: the teenager whose life would probably improve if he just hung on for six months, the terminally ill woman who most felt had a right to go, the elderly man who had lived a full life and wanted to join his departed spouse of sixty years. The teachers never mentioned what to do about the middle-aged adult who felt emptiness and despair despite support of loved ones, or was buckling under the weight of decades of joblessness.

Pete wasn't committable to a mental hospital against his will. By law he would have to be an immediate danger to himself or others. His suicide plans were only a remote eventual possibility. Even if he had been committed, under the present state system he would be out in a few days, more depressed and humiliated than before. More lengthy private psychiatric hospitalization might have provided adequate care. But that cost about $20,000 per month. Without insurance this route was impossible, given that he could not bring himself to burden his family with such an expense.

After two years of living with me, he decided to try to make a life in Las Vegas. He had some possible friend-of-a-friend contacts there. And the Las Vegas area was booming. His body was hurting nearly all the time in the humid Carolina mountain climate from his old car accident, and he felt that the desert heat might help with his arthritis. I remembered that he had joked when he came to live with me two years before that he would never commit suicide in my town, as it might damage my professional standing in the community. I worried that this last reason might be his strongest motivation for leaving. But I did not ask him point-blank about it, feeling that there was nothing positive to be said that hadn't been repeated many times. All of us who had come to know him in my town conveyed to him how much we treasured him. We made it clear that he would be welcomed joyfully, if he ever decided to return.

As Pete left for Las Vegas, I was greatly concerned that he would continue to hurt, but also hoped that things would be different for him there. I knew he had the potential to be an amazing worker if given a chance. He knew the gambling and hotel businesses well and would make an excellent personnel, hospitality, or gaming employee. He was ready to take a minimum wage job to start. But he was already so tired and beaten down.

With all his possessions packed into his car—now a worn, black, hand-me-down Ford sedan—he headed out after nervous smiles and heart-welling hugs were exchanged. Just as when he had left me at my parents' home to conquer life with his bride, once again swirling leaves suggested an ending of our close communion. This time we parted as men, knowing that men often hold wounds deep within the heart.

I sorely missed the delight of our daily contact. His quiet example and gentle love had nurtured my soul. But I was also relieved by his leaving. His pain, close at hand, was sharp and at the same time stiflingly heavy. It had been so hard to see him force himself up for each new job interview, put on the impeccable suit, pretend to be a winner, come home with hopes, and wait for the call to work that never came.

The initial news from Las Vegas was good. He liked desert living. It did help his arthritis. He let my folks "supplement his income," and he found a pleasant apartment with a pool. He was determined to relax and make a fresh start.

Time passed slowly for him, however. He continued to look for work vigorously, but his job hunting yielded nothing but growing disappointment. He discovered that in Las Vegas even convenience store clerks were credit-checked, and his past bankruptcy eliminated him from consideration.

I went to visit him in springtime. He seemed so pleased to see me and showed me the town. His apartment was bare, save a few pillows, a small TV, and a bed. He said he liked it that way. We took long walks with me gawking at the neon reds, blues, and greens dancing on hundred-foot signs. The contrast with country life couldn't have been more dramatic. He watched and advised as I gambled some, and we had many good laughs over my neophyte errors. Again I felt protected by him. It was wonderful to see him again—to remember that he was real.

Although not eagerly, Pete talked a little about his situation. He desperately wanted things to work out. I sensed that he was developing a timetable for his effort, with a deadline past which he would not go. Again the concern was that he would need more money from others, and he couldn't stand to take it. As I left, I felt his need for me and his isolation, although he bravely smiled. It was very hard to go.

As summer approached, the news worsened. When I called and pried it out of him, all he reported was a series of back-breaking straws. For example, he had landed a construction job on Friday. On Sunday he read in the newspaper that his new company was accused of unfair hiring. When he reported for work on Monday, they told him "Sorry." They had to hire minorities to get the press off their backs and could not use him at that time.

Soon after this incident, he called me to borrow five hundred dollars. He wanted to get his car running so he could date a girl who had asked him out. He sounded upbeat and eager for her company. I sent the money to him. She stood him up three times before he gave up on her. My family, friends, and the therapists I knew could give me no alternatives to present to him, aside from what he had already tried or what he had refused to try.

About a week after his son received his Master's degree, Pete called me on a Thursday. I wasn't home, and he told my wife it was not important. When I got home, she told me she was concerned. I called him, and we talked for a hour. I asked him if he needed help for car insurance, due the next day. He said he was going to let it lapse; he would renew it if he found work. He was friendly and warm, but kind of quiet. I promised to come out and see him again soon.

The following Monday night at about seven o'clock, I was home with my daughter watching TV when the phone rang.

"This is the Las Vegas police. Are you Joseph Gallenberger?"

"Yes."

"Your brother Pete is dead. It appears he committed suicide. Can we ask you some questions?"

"Who are you? Give me your number and I'll call you back."

"Certainly."

I ran upstairs, mind numb and heart racing. Maybe it was a creditor's scheme to track Pete down. Shaking, I dialed twice. I did not get through. I was more hopeful now, that this was a hoax. I dialed a third time carefully.

"Las Vegas police."

Oh, God. I am caught.

"Your brother shot himself with a thirty-eight in the right temple. It was a clean wound. I never have seen someone leave his apartment so clean. He left a note saying that he sold his car Friday and prepaid funeral expenses. He also sent a note to the funeral home telling them to pick him up at his address. He requested cremation and no funeral services. We were called to investigate. Your business card was found with instructions to call you. He has shipped all his belongings to your address. This is so considerate. You know most people who commit suicide in Las Vegas leave no identification and it's so hard to trace them. Did you know if he was depressed?"

"Yes, he was depressed."

"That's all we need to ask. Let us know who will be coming in to deal with his apartment. All that is left is his bed. He has cleaned out all the kitchen cabinets and refrigerator. He even took the sheets off the bed, put plastic down, and wrapped his head in a towel so as to not leave a mess."

I had to stop these inane comments about cleanliness. I had to stop the whole thing. I thanked him, asked if I could call him if I had questions, and hung up.

My six-year-old daughter Sarah, downstairs watching TV, was especially close to Pete. I started downstairs and reversed direction. I couldn't face her yet. I dialed my parents, fearing that they would hate me forever for telling them this news. My mother dropped the phone, wailing in grief. My father was stunned to silence. I shared what I knew and told him to go to Mother, that I would call the others and then call him back. I hung up and wept.

I called a neighbor who babysits Sarah; she agreed to come over. I told my daughter. She yelled, "No, That can't be! No,

No, No!" and "Why, Why, but Why?" and we rocked each other and wept. My neighbor arrived. She held us both. Then she took Sarah while I went back upstairs. I called my brothers and sister, Pete's girlfriend, and his ex-wife.

Pete's son, feeling a strong need to call his Dad and suspicious of all the busy signals, called my father and found out.

About two hours later, my wife came home, and I told her the news. Each telling slashed deep. Adrenaline still surging, we rushed to my office and searched his papers left in the basement—hoping for a letter or something. Midnight now, I called back my parents and brothers and plans were made. My eldest brother would go out, identify the body, and take care of things. I couldn't sleep and found myself at the computer, writing his eulogy. Nobody was going to mispronounce his name at the funeral or tell untruths about him.

My wife and I went through the next morning frantic and worn from too little sleep and too much stress. But that afternoon, while waiting to fly to my parents' home, we took a half-hour to meditate. A tremendous peace filled us both. There was no sense of contact with Pete, but more of an angelic consolation. The sunset flight was filled with beauty. Our serene mood lasted and spilled into peace for our family once we arrived.

Pete's son and I planned the services and what would be said, sitting under an oak in a park. I told him that I was never able to have a son and if he ever felt he needed a father . . . . He said he felt that he had three fathers now, in me and my two living brothers.

He and I went to the local priest and for my parents' sake we negotiated a full Catholic service, despite the suicide and cremation. We won but at a cost; I will always remember the discomfort of trying to explain my brother to the priest who sat in judgment. It felt like a violation to share intimate details with this stranger. I recall that part of what I said was that Pete was loving to everyone and yet in the end would have been happy to see the whole world blow up. The priest showed his uncomprehending disapproval. I wondered—didn't he sometimes get that frustrated?

The day of the funeral I woke up feeling a low but rising terror—a monster slowly waking within my gut. My daughter picked up my foreboding and didn't want to go. I feared I might die from grief, going through Pete's funeral. At the service, I saw my family ripped by sorrow. My daughter, thinking that she would throw up, left the church for a while with my wife. They returned as I delivered the eulogy.

A community of well-wishers waited in the back of the church, ready to console us. We didn't even register that they were there; we exited through the front of the church. We bled from the church to the gravesite, then we all went home—except my dear brother, Pete.

At my parents' home, we gathered with close friends. That afternoon we planted a Bradford Pear. It was Pete's favorite tree, and this specimen symbolized him well. It was not a sapling, but rather a strong, young, fifteen-foot-tall tree. It would have a delicate, lacy beauty in the spring when it bloomed with white flowers, but first it would meet fall wearing a strong ruddy crimson.

I saw my mother look out at the tree from the house later when daylight was waning. She said, "I can't wait to see it bloom next spring." Those words were sweet to hear, for I feared Pete's savage death would rob her of all determination to live. None of us there—mercifully—comprehended what it would take from us to live until spring.

PETE IS FREE OF TIME/SPACE
Eulogy for Pete

Dancing to Beach Boys
Flying the kite.
Lying in the sun here.
Enjoying a good joke.

Building book shelves
Out of block.
Pleasure and love
In simple living.

Fondness for cars
Kept shiny and bright.
Out-of-body excitement
Always aim for the light.

Roaming the mountains
On long limping walks.
Tending earth gently.
Harvesting sunflowers.

Teaching me Blackjack,
Poker, and people.
Always inviting me
To be my best.

Fiery curiosity
Old fashioned values.
Loving to family
Ever eager to serve.

Truest of friends.
Caring to strangers.
World's briefest letters.
Talks until two.

Sun-bronzed example
Of kindness, grace,
Endurance—
Yet couldn't keep pace.

Protecting us till now
From your great pain.
I love you, brother.
I need to see you again.

2 ∞ TURBULENCE

I didn't know that I could cry so much. And that tears would provide so little relief. Crying was just what I had to do. There was no control. The shock of suicide is total, yet shock only slightly buffers the pain. Denial steps in to help.

There is an intermixing of *It can't be* that extends long past the burial. Then the questions start: Why didn't he go back to college when he first found it difficult to get a job? Why did he have such a hard life when he was such a good man? Why didn't he keep trying? Why didn't someone help? How did we fail him? How did he fail life?

Pete's death was inconceivable from many angles. I had a six-year-old daughter who was closely attached to him—what was she feeling? Neither could I imagine what his suicide meant from his parents' perspective. I dwelled upon this often in those first few weeks and many times since. I have never dared ask them for a detailed, blow-by-blow description of their most private experience. My parents' loss remains unknowable.

Because he had lived with me and confided in me, and because of my background as a psychologist, many looked to me for answers. I had no real answers. I was drowning in my own questions.

My parents couldn't believe that he had been that depressed. I didn't know if it was more consoling to tell them of his decades of pain, so that his act made some sense, or to tell them less and let them think he acted out of temporary desperation. I voted to tell the truth as I saw it to anyone who asked. Truth seemed more important now, and secrets more deadly.

Family members called each other daily during those first few weeks. We pulled together. Living connections were appreciated anew. In the immediate family, no anger was expressed toward Pete. In-laws and others wondered out loud, "How could he do this to his dear parents?" That comment deeply offended me, even as I was beginning to brood, "How could he do this to me?"

Mostly, I felt that I had grievously failed him in some unclear way. I strove to renounce this feeling, knowing that I had loved him powerfully, intelligently, and consistently; but my feelings of guilt persistently slinked back into my being, time and time again.

Everyone in our family was careful to avoid even the hint of blame toward another. We shared ways we felt responsible. We reviewed what we had done—offering a place to stay, lending money, drumming up business connections, and visiting Pete. We knew that we had loved him. Now we agonized as to whether we had loved him in the correct way—the way that was best for him. We tried to wash away the stains of guilt for each other. Each knew that the others' actions did not cause this terrible act. But the stains would not vanish, only fade. My guilt first focused on wondering whether, by being both a friend and an unofficial therapist to him, I had ruined my chances at being useful to him as either.

I regretted that I had not gone to visit him again that summer. We all regretted unintentional rejections of him toward the end of his life—little things, such as saying "Can I call you back later?" and calling back within an hour; slight impatience with his urgent requests for us to follow up job leads, expressed as "I'm doing the best that I can. The person I need to contact for you is out of town." These were little, normal incidents, insignificant amid the consistent regard and support the family had extended him for so long; yet we recalled them in our agony.

During the years of trying to help him, I had tried to prepare for his possible suicide by telling myself that every human being has the right to decide whether to live, that his pain was deep and decades long, that his options were few, and that he deserved peace if he couldn't have success. But such thoughts would always be followed by revolt. He just had to make it! He was such a good man that somehow he would break through this impasse. After all—he was my hero.

A deeper secret began to surface. I perhaps had known when Pete was going to end his life. In the last weeks before his death, I had been unconsciously releasing him. How else to explain that I had become very dense for a perceptive individual trained as a therapist. I had missed the mounting signs that he was planning his death. I evidently acted upon my thoughts of helplessness and hopelessness about him. I acted by omission. I didn't struggle any longer to brace him up for yet another try at life. Now he had actually done it. He had killed himself.

After working as best I knew how to save him, in the end I had let him go without interference. I had let him know that my love and respect for him would endure, whatever he decided. In letting him go, had I committed the most terrible sin of my life by giving up on him? Or had I performed the most loving act of my life by granting him his freedom to choose? This was the kind of three-in-the-morning dilemma that could drive a person crazy. The question came between moments of restless sleep because during the day I didn't have time for it. I was mostly supporting everyone else and running away from the full impact of my own pain.

When I concentrated on Pete and focused past the brutal questions, it seemed that my heart went continually to our relationship: Who was he? Who was I? How were we the same? How were we different? The feeling that both of us were failures clouded out more positive memories during this time. I turned to writing and poetry to express my heart. I tried vainly to get my bearings in this storm of grief. I seemed to swirl with the randomness of a leaf in this whirlwind of bitter feelings and desperate questions.

Why did my brother have such bad luck? Was it luck, did he fulfill his fate, or was it consistent self-sabotage by a rebellious nonconformist? These questions seemed pivotal. It was obvious that he would still be around if his fortunes were different. He deeply enjoyed conversation, nature, helping others, and building things. He wanted to stay alive to experience all the wonders of this planet and of being human. But he couldn't find work.

The only explanation that made some sense was pure conjecture. He may have been suspicious of personal power. He could have been unconsciously so afraid that he would use it unwisely, or felt so undeserving of it, that he would not allow himself to gain even the minimum of personal power needed in order to live.

Many of us unconsciously limit our power to a level that is comfortable for us. Our society gives us such mixed messages about whether power is good or bad that sometimes we distrust the abundance that brings it. Some abuse their power so glaringly that we fear becoming like them, especially if we have been their victims in our youth. And now, in our culture, there is a deep distrust of male power in particular.

We start as children deeply wanting to please, to do well, and to enjoy power. But many raised in a perfectionist American and religious context begin to feel undeserving of true power and happiness. Most of us work out an uneasy compromise with these issues that allows us to live, although short of our full potential. Pete couldn't work out that compromise; he was never one to compromise principles.

It is curious that almost everyone who knew Pete felt that he was one of the most personally powerful people they had ever met. Without his saying anything, his mood would set the tone of the room; usually it was a wonderful tone of warmth and peace. He did countless good deeds that shaped others' lives. Yet he remained convinced of his own impotence. Much as the skeletal anorexic can look into the mirror and see a fat person, his self-perception was wildly divergent from reality.

I try to find lessons in Pete's experience. It helps make his death seem less senseless. His life suggests to me a message that earthly rewards don't necessarily come to the good. Abundance comes to those who feel entitled to it and take risks to allow their potency to grow. Goodness is of great value, and it is its own reward. But it is essential to feel deserving at a deep level for abundance, in the form of love, money, meaningfulness, or grace, to be fully received. Free will demands this. We are free to reject any or all benefit that could come to us. I try to raise my daughter to do good deeds *and* to feel worthy of all blessings, regardless of outside measures of performance.

The paradox of suicide emerges from its being at the same time the ultimate act of free will and the most radical surrender of will. Suicide can be an act of self-sabotage. But it can also be an expression of anger, a self-release, or a decision to go home. It often contains components of each. Its mystery is wrapped within the enigma of life and of death. Suicide penetrates deep into the nature of who we really are; it touches on issues of soul and spirit. And it brings up issues of life and afterlife.

Part of the dilemma of letting go of Pete is "What exactly must we surrender?" Clearly, he is no longer here in the physical. Obviously, we want to keep the good memories we have of him. Preferably, we can jettison the sorrow and defeat. Beyond these generalities, we enter unknown territory. Will we meet again in eternity? In our transformation, how much of our personality will be left—enough to know and care about each other? Religious and philosophical theories abound. Most suggest a going on—into heaven, or reincarnation, or as just a drop of consciousness added back into the cosmic ocean. Traditional science will have none of these approaches, but this matter is not within conventional science's domain. It is the realm of *spirit*, defined in the Random House Unabridged Dictionary as (1) the principle of conscious life; the vital principle in humans, animating the body or mediating between body and soul, and (2) the incorporeal part of humans.

So Peter died on July 15, 1991. As to the questions of why his life went the way it did, there are probably no clear answers known with certainty by anyone here.

Accessing the other side of the veil, if there is nonphysical existence, is difficult, but my brother's death demanded that I take a careful look into any source of information or experience that would shed light on what happened. My heart demanded that I seek contact with him and help him if it were possible. My compassion requires that I share what I found with others.

For the reader to understand why a modern man, trained as a scientist and psychologist, now *knows* that there is nonphysical life requires presenting considerable background. Please forgive the interruption of this story as I back up to do so in the next two chapters.

3 ∞ RECONNAISSANCE

After I read Pete's copy of *Far Journeys* by Robert Monroe, the out-of-body expert, I discovered that Monroe had started a research and educational facility in Virginia and offered workshops in changes of consciousness such as out-of-body experiences (OBE). The Monroe Institute also had home study tapes which could facilitate OBE and other meditative experiences.

I had been exposed to many other tapes in my work as a psychotherapist and, in fact, had for years used hypnosis in my practice when it was appropriate. I purchased some Monroe tapes and found them to be powerful. They were much different from standard relaxation and subliminal tapes, although they had some features in common with other tapes, such as verbal guidance and relaxing surf sounds. For me, Monroe tapes had a much deeper effect, allowing greater freedom and clarity during meditation and opening up new experiences of consciousness.

The tapes work through a principle now also used by other neuropsychological researchers, such as biofeedback expert Dr. Thomas Budzynski.[4] Sound is employed to lead the brain into special brain-wave rhythms associated with meditative states, much as waltz music is used to lead the dancer to waltz. These states are accomplished with great assistance from the Institute's patented sound-wave technology, called *Hemi-Sync®* for the hemispheric synchronization of the brain it encourages. One listens through headphones. Special tones help the brain learn to quickly balance its right and left hemisphere activity, and then to deeply relax. After relaxation is achieved, various states of consciousness are introduced and experienced.[5]

By the time I purchased the Monroe tapes, Pete was in pretty bad shape. He listened to the tapes a little, but found that he was too restless to relax during them.

In the spring of 1989 I went to The Monroe Institute's week-long introductory Gateway Voyage workshop. That week still ranks as the most profound of my life. To give a sense of what happened is difficult, but here are some highlights of the magic. On the way to the Institute I was so excited that I drove till 3 A.M. and stopped, exhausted, in the blackness of the Virginia countryside at a shoddy motel. I tried to sleep but was too excited and got up after an hour, waking up the sleepy clerk to check out.

As I left the building, I had the thought that I wished I didn't have to pay the $19.95 motel bill and immediately found a crisp, dry $20 bill, folded into thirds, lying on the cold damp outside step of the motel entrance. It was four in the morning. No one else was around, and I had looked at the same step just three minutes before on my way into the office. I never fold my own bills into thirds.

I arrived at The Monroe Institute later that morning to be greeted by Helen Warring, the Registrar, who was beaming excitement. She hugged me, laughing warmly, and showed me around the beautiful building and grounds. The Institute nestles into a knoll-top pasture in the Blue Ridge foothills, surrounded by taller peaks. Later that day, with twenty-four strangers and two trainers, I began an adventure in exploring consciousness that formed us all into life-long friends.

More than 7,000 participants worldwide have taken the Gateway Voyage, and it has been written about recently in the *Wall Street Journal*,[6] in *Omni* magazine,[7] and in many other books and periodicals such as *Healing Myself* by Gari Carter,[8] *Mind Trek* by Joseph McMoneagle,[9] and *Traveling with Power* by Ken Eagle Feather.[10]

Through the introductory Gateway Voyage program, one first must learn how to meditate deeply and to shed much fear of death. The program helps the participant do so through use of many Hemi-Sync tapes, through education and discussion, and through the gentle, accepting encouragement of the highly experienced Monroe trainers. As the participants free themselves from fear and unleash their creativity, many states of consciousness are explored.

The Institute uses numbers to designate these states to avoid previous associations to any names (such as "bliss" or "nirvana") given to these states by other disciplines. The state of balanced brain synchrony is referred to as Focus 3. Then one learns Focus 10, described as a state wherein the body is asleep or profoundly relaxed, while the mind is awake and alert. Few people realize that we can be highly conscious when completely relaxed or even while asleep. It is strange to feel wide awake and yet hear yourself snoring!

Next, the participant learns Focus 12, defined as a state where stimulation from the five physical senses is nearly absent or ignored, and information becomes more available through one's "sixth sense" or intuition. Here, participants often see visions and hear voices which do not exist in physical reality. Sometimes information is obtained through an instant knowing. Communication with one's own unconscious becomes much more available. Nonphysical energies (whether termed the Higher Self, guides, angels, or God) often "speak" to the person through words, images, or knowings in Focus 12. This state is probably most similar to deep prayer and mystical states enjoyed by the devout. There is often a great deal of humor and creativity in these exchanges. These impressions can be subtle or intensely vivid.

In Gateway Voyage, one then moves on to Focus 15 consciousness. This is defined as a freeing from all adherence to the construct of time. Linear thought ceases. Everything seems to be occurring in an eternal now. Other disciplines refer to this state as experiencing the Void, both everything and no-thing, or the point of infinite potentiality. It is often blissful. In this state of consciousness, one can move through time easily, back to the past—or receive glimpses of the future.

Gateway Voyage concludes with teaching people how to experience Focus 21 consciousness. This is harder to describe. One can think of it as a bridge between physical and nonphysical reality. It is usually experienced somewhat like the bright light of near-death experiences and with the same sense of profound peace and safety. In this state, communication with loved ones who are deceased, as well as with other nonphysical "friends" is often clear and complete.

In my group, there were participants from around the world: three from Australia, one from Denmark, and two from Canada. Most were peaceful but powerful, multi-talented introverts. They were passionate and knowledgeable talkers if approached one-on-one. Many worked in the information or engineering fields, others in consulting or the healing professions.

The trainers' talks centered upon reducing our fears of the unknown and suggested we suspend struggle, impatience, and competing to have the most interesting experiences. They encouraged us to be willing to playfully explore new perceptions. During the program, listening to Hemi-Sync tapes resulted in much more profound relaxation and higher energy states than when I used them at home prior to coming to the Institute.

I experienced a variety of OBE states during Gateway Voyage, as well as clear knowledge of contact with intelligences much greater than my own conscious mind. It was as if I repeatedly prayed and received back as clear a message as I had sent. This bathed me in blissful and loving feelings. I felt my compassion for others expanding and even felt this physically as a dinner-plate-size warm glow over my heart area.

My fellow travelers and I became increasingly intuitive and then often what I can only call telepathic. During a tape exercise, I would suddenly become aware of another participant's presence in my mind. In these deep meditative states it was easy to relate with the other persons, to instantly know important things about them, to pass thoughts, feelings, and tremendous energy back and forth, and to understand one's connections with them that often included past lives together. The program changed forever how I viewed myself and the world.

When I returned home, Pete listened to my experiences at the Institute with great interest and some skepticism. He renewed his own efforts, and he found that he could occasionally induce the OBE state for himself by trying to remain conscious as he fell asleep. But, whereas I experienced the exhilaration of freedom from the physical body and found upon returning that the physical world was more pleasing and exciting as well, OBE experience was different for Pete. He used it to escape his physical and emotional pain and was understandably savaged by the return—much as when we awaken from a beautiful dream to confront some ugly reality.

My Gateway Voyage immediately created great changes in my life. Results flowered on many levels—from an increased self-awareness to a winning attitude. At times it got pretty spooky. For example, within the first few months of attending Gateway Voyage, I won several contests, including a prize of thousands of dollars worth of compact discs and stereo equipment. This was particularly sweet because music is one of the greatest joys of my life.

I was concerned that the effects of the Gateway Voyage would wear off. I had been to many seminars where one became flushed with enthusiasm and insight, only to become "normal" within weeks of returning home. Voyage was different. For me it seemed to start a catalytic reaction that continued to increase in depth as time went by.

That summer I attended The Monroe Institute's graduate program, Guidelines[11] and found it also of great value. Soon after, I became a trainer of Monroe programs both at the Institute and in my local community. I liked the fact that there was no dogma that one had to accept in order to benefit from the programs. And the Institute's sound technology made it relatively easy to reach deep meditative states that had eluded me during decades of standard meditation practice.

This affiliation with The Monroe Institute energized my life. It lifted the residuals of depression and enhanced my creativity. So, in one way it widened the gap between my brother's experience and mine, as he was still stuck and suffering. Yet it also deepened our bond. Pete was highly interested in my dramatic changes and very curious about the "other side"— possible nonphysical realities and peak states of consciousness.

Therefore, we had something fascinating and fresh to talk about, as opposed to continually problem-solving about his situation.

My wife also joined our conversation because she was attending Institute programs as well and having her own amazing stories to tell. Pete, in his graciousness and acceptance, was becoming a brother to her. He fed her deep desire for family fellowship. And he supported her venturing forth into the new areas she was exploring, such as Karate and public speaking.

Given how much I benefited from Gateway Voyage, I strongly encouraged Pete to go to one himself. He declined—I think for at least four reasons: (1) his experience with tapes at home had produced only restlessness; (2) he was a private person by nature and felt such shame about his situation by then that revealing himself to strangers was not a pleasant prospect; (3) he was not comfortable with what he thought would be an atmosphere where hugging and the word "love" would be bandied about freely; and (4) he felt that he couldn't spend the money it would have cost to go, even if the family had chipped in to provide it.

I still wish that he had gone and wonder if it would have made the key difference. I know that his privacy would have been respected, that his situation and his person would have been accepted, and that the money was unimportant relative to his own value. Perhaps in a week-long setting with the support of others, he would have been able to let down his guard and move into the open states encouraged by the program. All I can do is accept that either it was not meant to be, or that it was just too uncomfortable for him to attempt.

In one of the strangest synchronistic mysteries of life and death that Pete and I are sharing, I had just returned from The Monroe Institute's first offering of a program called Lifeline and had also recently trained Pete's son in a weekend mini-Gateway Voyage when I received the call that Pete had died.

Lifeline is a program designed to teach one in deepest meditation how to help the dying or the dead make their journey safely to the other side—pretty wild stuff! That is quite an assertion for me to make, and I think I owe the reader more of an explanation of how such a thing might work.

Again, Lifeline is a graduate program. To prepare for it, first one must take the Gateway Voyage program. The Lifeline program assumes that one is familiar with accessing the states of consciousness already referred to as Focus 3 through Focus 21. Lifeline's purpose is to help the experienced meditator access deeper realms of nonphysical reality for the purpose of helping others in those realms. And in doing so, the person learns much about his or her greater self and the nature of higher realities.

To describe Lifeline is a bit complicated. Lifeline starts with a quick review of the lower focus levels and then, through different brain-wave signals, facilitates the exploration of Focus 22. This is the state of "dissociated consciousness" where dreams and strong drug experiences take place. When in a Focus 22 meditative state, one can also communicate with the consciousnesses of people who are in coma. It is more "there" than "here."

Lifeline then helps its participants to experience Focus 23. This state is defined as the vibration or phase of consciousness of those who are newly deceased and not yet released from the physical plane. We can call them "new goners" rather than "new comers"—the universe allows a sense of humor. In some systems Focus 22 and 23 are referred to as the lower and higher astral planes. It is here that one "meets" souls who are needing assistance to move on.

Often those who need assistance have experienced violent or unexpected death. Some do not realize yet that they are dead. They seem caught in the emotional shock/trauma of their passing. Thought seems to be reality in this state. So his thinking can deceive the person into believing that he is still alive in the physical. Again, most people die and transition to a new existence quite easily, depending on their faith. It is rare that a soul needs assistance of the type provided by Lifeline. But given that about a half-million people die each week on planet Earth, there is ample need for such assistance.

Lifeline next presents Focus 24 through 26. These are the "belief system" areas where consciousness is narrowly focused on a particular idea of an after-life, such as nirvana or heaven. Finally, Focus 27, the farthest reaches of consciousness that still has primarily human characteristics, is experienced and the Park is introduced. The Park is a place within Focus 27 designed to make newly deceased persons feel comfortable. There one is surrounded by everyday, Earth-like images such as trees and buildings.

After the meditator is familiar with these higher Focus levels (22 to 27), he (or she) is trained to go rapidly to Focus 27 and ask for a nonphysical helper to assist him. He then goes with this assistant back to Focus 23 and waits till he feels pulled to connect with a consciousness in need of his help. When contact is made, the meditator helps the consciousness calm down, orient to the fact of his death, and offers to take him to the Park by linking energies and willing himself back to Focus 27. There the meditator leaves the deceased person in the "hands" of loved ones or helpers.

As can be imagined, this is a very interesting process and stretches what one thinks is real and possible. To me, Focuses 12 through 21 feel wonderful—each in its own way light, calm, and free. In contrast, Focus 22 and 23 feel chaotic and "darker." But Focus 27 and the Park feel incredibly clear, clean, and peaceful. It is as if there is no mental chatter there. The Park for me is experienced in detail with beautiful flowers, grass, ponds, and trees. While Focuses 12 through 21 are powerful mind states, they do not feel physical. Focus 27, on the other hand, feels like I am in a Shangri-La on Earth. Strangely, when you are at any focus level you may spontaneously "meet" a fellow meditator there, and when you get back independently confirm your joint experience.

When you wait in Focus 23 for someone in need, it seems as if nothing is going on. Then you feel a pull, like the pull that causes you to turn your head to find someone staring at you. You then "see" a situation—for example, a person killed in a motorcycle accident. That person may be trying to pick up her bike over and over, with her hands passing right through the bike. She is confused and often frightened or angry. You approach and ask if you can help. She notices you sometimes only after considerable effort to get her attention. You can hear her thoughts. You can feel her emotions. In your high, calm meditative state, her emotions feel low-energy and painfully agitating. You don't really speak, you just read each other's thoughts. It may go something like this:

"Can I help?"

"I can't get this damn bike up!"

"What happened?"

"A stupid drunk ran me right off the road and into that tree."

"What are you doing?"

"I got to get to school—have a big test today."

"You may not be able to."

"Why the hell not?"

"What did you feel when you hit the tree?"

There is now a strong sense of pain and fear radiating off this person.

"I hurt all over and then I was fine."

"Don't you think that is a little strange?"

"Come to think of it, yes."

"You may feel good now because you've changed. See your body over there?"

"Yes. What's happening? Am I dead? I don't feel dead. I can move and everything."

"Of course, only your body dies; you don't die."

"I can't be dead. I'm too young."

"Now, stay calm and think it through. Could you have survived hitting that tree?"

"No . . . my God! What do I do now?"

"Well, you can come with me."

"Where?"

"I'll take you to a place where you can rest and think. There will be people there to help you, perhaps even someone you know."

"OK."

"Just hang on to my hand and stay with me. Here we go."

Other people have been in Focus 23 for a while by Earth-time standards, for there is really no time outside of physical reality. When I was leading a Lifeline program, one participant reported coming across a man who seemed very low in energy. She knew him and knew that he had died a few years before. He seemed to realize that he was dead.

She asked, "Hasn't anyone been by to help you?"

He replied, "There have been many beautiful angels coming by but I have hidden from them."

She asked why he would do this.

"Because they were going to take me to judgment and I don't want to go." She was able to help him move on only after considerable assurances to him. This situation points to how our beliefs may cause us to get stuck after we die.

Young children who have died while being severely abused are often very hard to reach—their fear is so great. Sometimes other souls are so angry or distressed that the meditator simply cannot tolerate the emotional radiations emanating from the person. The meditator cannot get close enough to help. Yet this emotional distress may be one reason that nonphysical intelligence needs the help of Earth-bound meditators to work with the souls of some of the dead. If physically alive meditators have trouble handling the agitation, perhaps nonphysical energies of an even finer vibration just can't penetrate the dense agitation of the distressed. There are certain meditators that specialize in difficult areas, such as working with victims of Satanic cults.

The easiest retrievals are often elderly people who have been ill a long time. The following dialogue is typical of these situations:

After entering Focus 23 during meditation, I felt a pull and found myself at the foot of a bed in a hospital.

"Oh, thank God you're here. What took you so long? All my pain has stopped. Boy that feels good! I'm ready to go."

"Fine. I'll help you."

"Could I ask a favor?"

"Sure."

"Could we just go by the hotel across the street? I want to say goodbye to my wife."

"Sure. Just remember to keep holding my hand"

Then, as we progressed to Focus 27, I asked some questions. To these questions I received impressions. For example, to the question "Where are you from?" I received a rapid series of pictures of a modest middle-class house, his favorite cat, his children, the inside of his living room, and the words "Dayton, Ohio."

At this time about 500 meditators, in groups of twenty-four at a time, have gone through the Lifeline program. There have been efforts to verify some of the experiences by researching whether someone died with the name and in the manner and time that the meditator reports. There have been several confirmations.

Perhaps the program sounds grim, with its focus on helping people still reacting to the pain and violence of death. On the contrary, participants are usually very joyous because they often experience the intense delight of reunions on the other side between loved ones in the Park and the new arrival.

My experience with my own mother provides an example of the beauty of this process. I had been concerned that her intense feelings of guilt and strong fears of Judgment Day would cause her to have difficulty passing smoothly through the process of her own death. I was not immediately anticipating my mother's death, so my concern was out of my awareness most of the time; but it was there fairly constantly nonetheless.

Lifeline retrievals involve operating in nonphysical states, where time does not exist as we know it. They usually occur in the present, but they are actually free of time constraints. Therefore, it may be possible within these meditations to tap into situations that will occur in the future. Of course, there is no way to verify such experiences—at least until Earth time catches up with them! The adventure with my mother may involve such a time-jump; on the other hand, this experience may have been a simulation, designed to help me with two concerns. The first, of course, was my worry that my mother would have difficulty passing over when the time came. This adventure replaced that anxiety with a sense of deep peace, a trust that she will successfully transition when she eventually dies. Secondly, the information I had read about Lifeline at this point, prior to any experience with it, was so foreign to my belief systems that it triggered concern. I worried that the Lifeline process may not be possible, or at least may not be possible for *me* to accomplish. My experience with my mother showed me how such a process can work and what it might feel like.

This experience occurred about two weeks before I participated in the Lifeline workshop, bringing my reading about the Park to life. One day, after ten hours of client work, I was extremely tired and lay down to rest and meditate. As I moved deeper into the meditative state, I felt pulled into the future. The experience went something like this:

I felt that I was at the opposite end of the tunnel that people describe in near-death experiences. Someone was coming through. I recognized that it was my mother. I calmed myself. She seemed to begin to recognize me. I felt the beginnings of her confusion at seeing me (from her point of view I was not supposed to be there) before she was even conscious of recognizing me. I masked my identity at once—surprised that I could do this. I beamed out radiations of peace and love. She immediately calmed down and moved forward. I greeted her. She asked:

"Are you an angel?"

"I'm here to help you."

"Have I died?"

"I guess you have left your body."

"Can I go with you?" (I felt she had doubts about her worthiness).

I beamed acceptance, support, and love. "Sure you can. I will take you where you need to go."

I didn't know what to do next and felt a little panicky. Instantly the thought occurred to me that in this state I could create reality. I put some roses in her hand, knowing that she loved flowers. She brightened instantly and seemed absorbed with the roses. This diversion gave me a split-second to think.

Ah! I sent her the thought-form of a newborn baby. Immediately a baby appeared in her arms and I felt a radiation of tremendous love off of her. We stayed this way for a while.

Then something else seemed to take over the scene. I seemed no longer in control. The baby became me. I felt her love for me as an infant. I sent her memories of all the loving times we had had together: running through freshly hung wet sheets till I found her and hugged her legs—reminded her how she stopped her work, picked me up, and hugged me till I laughed with delight. I let her see her devoted smile through my child eyes. Dozens of memories flooded through me and to her. I had the thought that I was helping her with her life-review and that that was the right thing to do. During this while, I was also willing us to travel to the Park. I was entranced at watching her life review as the baby in turn became each of her children.

Suddenly I was aware of another presence with us. It was her mother. The bliss of their reunion overwhelmed me as I felt their emotion. I steadied myself as best I could, feeling their joy myself. Others joined us—I recognized her father and sisters. The feelings just kept mounting to new heights of ecstasy. It was the ecstasy of love unbounded, of coming home, of true safety at last.

I began to realize that my part was done and began to move away. As I did so, and their radiations faded, I began to feel the loss of my mother and was at once overcome with grief at the rending. I cried out for help and instantly felt a calming presence that guided me back to consciousness of the physical with great gentleness and love. In clock time, thirty minutes had passed. My sense that we live in an intelligent and planned universe—loving beyond our bounds of understanding—becomes forever my knowing.

So the experience of helping on the other side profoundly changes the meditator. After several experiences, the participants know that they are much more than their physical selves, and understand much more about the love, intelligence, and beauty that exists everywhere in the universe—on both sides of the veil.

By now I suspect that my readers will have some important questions which I will attempt to anticipate.

What are other possible explanations for what is going on in the Lifeline program?

There seems to me to be no possibility of fraud. I have experienced the process directly myself, not just heard reports of it. It also seems very unlikely that it is some form of group hysteria, for several reasons. The process occurs spontaneously on an individual basis (for example, the experience I had helping my mother, which occurred a few weeks before the first Lifeline group even met); experiences have occurred in those who are very skeptical of the process, such as professed atheists, and there has been independent verification of the facts collected concerning the circumstances of some of the deaths.

But before concluding that Lifeline represents, at least at times, actual contact and interaction with humans who are no longer on the physical plane, two other explanations need to be explored. One possibility is that somehow the meditators are picking up the emotional-mental echoes left behind after the person has died. The problem with this idea is that the experience is so interactive. It is not fragmentary. It is not like "listening to a broken record." Another idea is that some nonphysical intelligence uses the meditator's own unconscious to gather information and then simulates being the soul that needs help. This idea also seems unlikely in that often the meditator is pulled to work with perfect strangers rather than loved ones, and the process yields information that the meditator does not previously know and which can be verified.

Could this process be evil or unnatural?

I discussed the process with a fundamentalist Christian friend. He felt that anything psychic was evil and that if these meditators were communicating with anything, it was with demons. He was sincerely concerned for my welfare, and I appreciated his concern. However, I believe in the Biblical adage "By their fruits you shall know them." Because of the meditators' uniformly positive and integrative reactions to their work and because of the tremendous feelings of love and inspiration experienced, I am very confident that this represents a "gift of the spirit."

Why would I, as a trained clinical psychologist, give credence to any process that claims to be able to reach beyond death?

I can say with scientific certainty that distinct meditative states exist and that sound, by affecting brain waves, can induce these states. I can point to work being done at advanced physics and engineering laboratories, such as Princeton Engineering Anomalous Research Laboratory,[12] and previous work at Duke University and Stanford University which suggests that human consciousness is not dependent on physical matter. This body of research also suggests that we can move through time, perceiving and affecting events in the past and future.

I can offer Charles Tart's article "Compassion, Science and Consciousness Survival[13] as a good summary of evidence for the survival of consciousness after death. I can also point to the aeons of intuition embedded in religions, that submits that we exist after physical death.

I know that what occurs in Lifeline is practiced in a variety of forms in other disciplines such as shamanism. Christians and others pray for their dead, seeking to aid their loved one's progress toward peace and to God.

What I cannot do is point to scientific proof of either an afterlife or the Lifeline process. But I feel that is the deficiency of science, not the data. Science at this time is restricted to the at-least-indirectly observable. Questions of afterlife go beyond its ken. Science is valid, but there are other ways to find truth as well—ways such as through mutually verified experiences and through the human heart. Furthermore, the concept of how one can pierce the veil and what one can do there is consistent with leading-edge science in the field of quantum physics.

Why is such tremendous news not more widely known?

First, much of the data and scientific conclusions to which I refer to are very recent (occurring within the past ten years). Secondly, traditional science is capable of behaving as a religion when confronting new thought: it suppresses data that doesn't agree with its current belief system, chiefly by ignoring it.

True story: I am aware of a prestigious university laboratory that completed an exhaustive, fully-controlled study that showed that humans can affect physical matter through thought alone. When the researchers sought publication in a peer review journal, they were told, "When you can send us the data by telepathy we will look at it." Inability to publish equals inability to get major funding.

Thirdly, the scientists doing this work are often very introverted by nature and fear they would be thrown out of their universities if they went to the popular press. Most universities tolerate this type of inquiry under the principle of academic freedom only if it is kept quiet, meaning no "wild" claims are made.

Why do I feel comfortable trusting The Monroe Institute?

It is primarily due to my extensive personal experience with the place. I have used The Monroe Institute as an extensive example here because it is a unique institution, a nonprofit "university" studying human consciousness. In my opinion it is at the leading edge in its field. It is a place where the farthest reaches of the human mind are explored and where what is learned is taught compassionately. In that special atmosphere of intelligence and love, great creativity and human potential flower.

While the Institute's budget is fairly small, its ethics and dedication are above reproach. It accepts no government funds. There is no guru there. There is no agenda of power or greed. It has a stellar board of advisors, and more than a hundred professional members, including many Ph.D.s and M.D.s. Its tape technology is being studied by major universities such as the University of California at Davis (for its use in surgery) and the University of Virginia (for its usefulness in healing). At the time of this writing, I understand that The National Institutes of Health are interested in exploring Hemi-Sync's potential in medicine. For further detail about many uses of Hemi-Sync, I refer the reader to the book *Using the Whole Brain,* edited by Ronald Russell,[14] which contains more than forty articles on the application of Hemi-Sync in education, medicine, and meditation.

The Institute's use of valid principles of reverse engineering—using brain-wave patterns of talented subjects to create new Hemi-Sync signals—puts it at the cutting edge in assessing, duplicating, and teaching specialized brain-wave states that are at the current limits of human potential. The Institute possesses its own research division which has a 24-lead EEG neuromapper and other physiological monitoring equipment and is dedicated to objective reporting of results.

Perhaps my readers can't accept everything that I am suggesting. But it is my truth, derived through my own background, training, and experience. (I should add the disclaimer that my words are my own opinions and not necessarily those of The Monroe Institute.) All I ask is that one keep an open mind. Remembering that the best way to know anything is to directly experience it, perhaps the best that my readers can do, as my story progresses, is to see if what I am saying is logical, coherent, consistent. And discover whether it resonates not with what you have been taught, but with your own mind, heart, and experience.

The night Pete died, when I went to my office to search for a note from him (or probably to run away from the place where I had heard the news), I called one of the trainers of that first Lifeline that I had attended just the week before and asked her to go look for Pete on the other side and help him if she could. Teena graciously agreed to try to help. I wanted to search for Pete myself, but loved ones immediately after experiencing a death are usually too agitated to meditate that deeply; I was no exception. The following are experts from my personal journal written at the time.

7/17/91   Teena's Report:

[I called Teena 11:00 P.M. 7/15/91, the night of Pete's death and asked her to find and help Pete. Teena is experienced in soul rescue work. She feels that, going into an altered state of consciousness, she can contact the part of us that survives physical death. She called me back the next day.]

Teena reports that she easily found Pete on the nonphysical plane. That he was glad to see someone who recognized him. His energy was scattered. In deep meditation, she spent about twelve hours with him, helping him to gather himself together, to calm down and to focus.

She introduced him to Focus 27 guides. He is surrounded by many protecting spirits. Focus 27 is The Monroe Institute term for the highest plane that still has relationship to human existence. Located in Focus 27 is a place called The Park, that was constructed and is maintained through human mental creativity, to duplicate the environment of Earth on a nonphysical plane of existence.

The Park is used to help souls newly released from the physical body to calm down in a familiar environment. These souls then can rest, review their lives, and make decisions about what to experience next. Some souls appear to choose to go to their idea of heaven, some to reincarnate. Other options also exist. Many souls go directly into heaven or another physical life without ever going through The Park. It is a place designed more to help those who are unaware that they are dead, are confused, or who have no strong prior belief system in a given afterlife.

Teena said that the main thought Pete sent her was that he was so happy to be out of the physical. By the end of this initial twelve-hour period he was calmer. He really wants to make contact with me. He really wants to talk to me. He is doing fine and is plugged into a very nice healing process. He was humorous about the traumatic energy that was released by the shooting, commenting, "That was not the way to make an easy transition."

Teena recommends that, for me to make contact with him, I should slow down [I was very upset at the time], get comfortable, and allow myself to feel subtle energy and sensations. Just allow the process to happen and stay aware of nuances. That I am powerfully psychic but need to calm down and open up. [It was after receiving this report that I took the half-hour to meditate before taking the plane to Pete's funeral and felt the great sense of peace that gentled my family's initial grieving.]

7/19/91 Teena's report:

[Teena again contacted Pete five days after his death, at my request.]

"At this time Pete is more involved with whom he needs to be involved with—undergoing a group orientation. He is losing attachment to the physical quickly. He is working on what has been learned in this life. He is engaging in much remembering of all that he is beyond his immediate last Earth incarnation. He is very comfortable with everyone's acceptance of his transition and feels very good about that acceptance. He was concerned about his loved one's reactions. He will continue to be available—more so as he integrates his energy."

Teena feels that this is an excellent opportunity for me, and that I am getting communication from him on an unconscious level. To make communication more conscious, I need to let go of a screen of beliefs that are in the way and be aware of the subtle stuff.

I questioned Teena: "What is in the way?"

She responded, "Traditional understandings of how the mind works stand in the way. Usually what one is best at in the physical gets in the way in this type of communication. You, Joe, are best at understanding the mind and have many conceptions as a psychologist about how the mind works. Loosen your preconceptions for a while. Let go of the need to understand for a while and just perceive.

"Pete at this time is very honed in on what we are thinking of him. He can easily understand us and 'see' what is going on. He is trying to extend thoughts of peace, love, and fun. Also, he wants to convey that he has experienced a state change, that it is not life versus death. That there really is no separation, that he is still connected and we are with him."

7/20/91 Lu's Report:

[Lu, a member with me in the first Lifeline group, had had many years' experience with psychic impressions before attending Lifeline. She had not been informed of Pete's suicide, but she called five days after his death.]

Lu called me, unsolicited, saying that Pete had some messages for me. She felt that he had suicided and had been ill for a long time. She saw him dressed in soft gray slacks and shirt. That he looked good. He wanted his parents to know that his way of life had been chosen beforehand. He stated, "Do not grieve. Time is nonessential. Life exists forevermore."

She saw rays of light emanating from his hands and heard the thought, "I am sending my family love, strength, and health." Lu saw a heavy gold ring with a large square stone in it. She also got the feeling "release me." Lu got the impression that for Pete, it will not be necessary to re-live this life. That even though there was a suicide, he is released from repeating this life's experience because he had been in such pain for so long with very restricted options. He will learn the lessons needed without re-experiencing them in the physical.

Even with what I feel is a decent amount of scientific support for the principles involved, and this data coming out of association with a reputable organization, The Monroe Institute, my skeptical mind still sought independent confirmation of the things being said about Pete and the after-life. The next chapter introduces the background for that part of my journey.

4 ∞ GUIDANCE

When Pete came to live with us, he brought another exotic experience into our lives. He told us of a channeler in Ohio named Pam Hogan. Pam (who had no affiliation with The Monroe Institute) allowed a nonphysical energy to speak through her while she was in a trance state. Pete had heard that she would give a one-hour reading by telephone, with the caller giving no information besides his first name. She would be extremely accurate as to one's life situation and predictions concerning the future. This was before channeling became more well-known, and to believe that such a thing was possible was a stretch of our belief systems and felt dangerous from our Catholic and scientific perspectives. We were skeptical but intrigued.

Pete and I had separate channeled sessions, and I have had many readings since. I am not sure what to make of these sessions, but several excerpts from them speak to what happened with Pete and with me.

But first a brief digression about the phenomenon of channeling . . .

There appear to be at least three ways to get information during deep meditation. In the first, the person goes into meditation, has an experience, comes back to normal consciousness, and reports it. In the second way, an experienced mediator learns to talk while in a deep meditative state and report what is going on as it happens. This is particularly useful because many meditative experiences fade quickly after returning to normal consciousness, much as a vivid dream can fade upon awakening. In this meditative condition, if the experience is one of communicating with another intelligence, the person can report the dialogue while it is actually occurring. The third way information is obtained involves the meditator allowing the intelligence with whom he or she is communicating to speak directly to a listener (who is in normal waking consciousness and can record what is said). Here the meditator lets his own personality or ego fade and permits the other intelligence to use the meditator's own vocabulary and vocal cords to express thoughts directly. This third way of getting information is called *channeling.*

Some channelers report "going somewhere else in consciousness" while this is happening and have vivid and separate experiences while the channeling is going on. This type of channeler has little or no memory of what is said by the intelligence who is communicating. Other channelers are conscious of what is being said during the meditation. These are referred to as *conscious channels.* Pam Hogan is a conscious channel.

The phenomenon of channeling is now being studied neurophysiologically through brain-wave analysis. Most reputable channelers when channeling exhibit a distinct and unusual brain-wave pattern. The pattern is consistent with deep meditation. Several books now out are reported to be channeled works, including the copious Seth material,[15] the Emmanual Books,[16] the Michael material,[17] and *A Course in Miracles.*[18]

There is much debate about the reality of the phenomenon. The first option to consider is that it is faked. This possibility is unlikely due to the rapidness and complexities of answers to questions spontaneously posed and to the accuracy of information otherwise known only to the questioner. Furthermore, the brain-wave patterns of a monitored channeler are very different from what one would expect from a person consciously faking.

If the phenomenon isn't a pretense, what *is* this other intelligence that is contacted? Some speculate that it is the channeler's own unconscious mind. But the channeler often speaks in a way that differs considerably from what one might expect if the unconscious were driving the thoughts; in other words, channeling does not proceed in a manner similar to either Freudian free-association or hypnotic speech.

Other skeptics hypothesize that the channeler accesses his own supraconscious mind, which then may access Carl Jung's Universal Unconscious—the human collective intelligence. This explanation would account for the cogency of answers. However, channelers are convinced that they access and relate with another intelligence or group of minds that have their own personality and higher emotions such as love, concern, and compassion. With repeated sessions, channelers often come to know and love the other intelligences, relating much as one might to good friends. What these intelligences say about themselves is that they exist outside of normal physical reality and that some have experienced physical life at some time.

Most channelers report that it is important to move into this skill carefully and to always be discerning regarding the quality of the other intelligence and be in dominion concerning one's own life choices. They feel that playing around with a Ouija board, for example, with the intention of contacting another intelligence, can instigate contact with intelligences that are of fairly low-quality motivation. These energies may pretend to be a loved one, gaining information through a telepathic link with the channeler, or may seek to control the channeler and live vicariously through the channeler's life experience. Channelers feel that they can determine the motivation of the intelligence through a sense of the energy's power and love, and the constructiveness of advice and perceptions given over time.

An interesting variant of channeling is having nonverbal information pour through without conscious control. Handel felt his personality was moved aside and that angels directly wrote the music to *The Hallelujah Chorus*. Many other artists have reported similar experiences, that their inspiration came from somewhere outside of themselves. In fact, there are now channelers living who seem to be directly accessing the skills of some of the greatest painters and musicians who have ever lived. It is reported that highly skilled art critics who are trained

to detect forgeries often claim that the channele
indistinguishable from the styles of, for exampl
or Bach.

Pam Hogan, who has relocated to Taos, New м........,
she first crossed my path, is by far the highest-quality channeler
whom I have directly encountered. She communicates with a
nonphysical intelligence she named ARGO for Ascending Rays
of God's Oneness. Pam has a degree in social work and worked
as a traditional therapist before starting to offer readings. Her
story is an interesting one and can be found outlined in the
Appendix of this book. But now let's return to the story of
Pete and me.

My initial session with Pam was highly individualized and
extremely accurate as to central issues of my life. There were
very few statements that I could dismiss as applying generally
to everyone. It was also 100-percent accurate in predictions
made for the behavior of gold and a few stocks. These predictions were specific as to exact dates that prices would rise and
for how long the rise would continue. And most of these
predictions went against conventional market wisdom at that
time. With Pete's encouragement, I bought some stock options
following the channeler's advice and acquired some of the most
exciting money I have ever made! I was impressed by—and
mention here—the market predictions because they were sci-
entifically verifiable. Unless one was going to accuse Pam of
insider trading in several companies simultaneously and of
fixing the international market in gold, it was hard not to be
in awe of the quality of this information.

More important was how I felt after this first session. There
was a tremendous sense of energy and well-being that extended
for about a week after the session. I felt that I was being filled
with grace or being prayed for by a powerful angel.

In subsequent sessions, I encountered a reluctance to give
more financial information. The exception to this was warnings
about when the market was about to take a serious downward
turn, apparently given to allow me to protect my self-admin-
istered pension fund. These subsequent predictions were usually

not always accurate. I have the sense that the initial specific market predictions were given to get the attention of the scientist in me so that I would listen and consider more important messages concerning the direction and meaning of my life.

The channeled readings which I received before Pete's death give insight into the deeper aspects of my brother's life. The excerpts presented here have been edited for increased clarity but left essentially in their original form. Given that they represent communication from a nonphysical intelligence or entity—beyond the veil, if you will—I ask for tolerance of the somewhat odd style of expression. Such unusual language is common to all channeled material of which I am aware, including those in the works cited above.

Sometimes Pam puts her impressions in her own words. At other times Pam lets ARGO speak directly through her without her conscious control. I think of ARGO as an angel, for want of a better word, due to the lovingness and wisdom of the message. I find that talking with ARGO is profoundly different than talking with a typical human person. I have never sensed the qualities of wandering attention, triviality, impatience, judgment, criticism, hostility, or defensiveness—so common in human communication—when speaking with ARGO. Instead, ARGO communicates with consistently exquisite discernment in an atmosphere of full attention and compassion.

Another startling difference is that ARGO responds not only to what I am saying but also to what I am thinking deep within my heart—and it may be an exact response to what I was thinking yesterday or will think in the future. ARGO does not always say what I want to hear. For example, when I had completed my first novel, I excitedly asked how it would do. The response I got was that it would not be immediately successful, but that its writing was good preparation for doing a second book. This prediction turned out to be true.

I listen carefully to the channelings, but I swallow nothing whole and at times have gone against recommendations. My feeling is that just because intelligences may be discarnate ("dead") doesn't mean they are infallible or always right. This attitude seems fine with ARGO. Free will and personal sovereignty seem highly respected. Additionally, as in any communication, there is a possibility of distortion—what is said may not be what is meant, and what is said may not be what is heard. There are at least three sources of potential error in channeled information: error in the intelligence communicating; error through the channeler's mediumship; and error in the receiver's understanding of what is heard. I found, however, that when I went against the channeled guidance there would frequently be less-desired outcomes. Yet those experiences were also useful for my continued learning and growth. The school of hard knocks is an effective way to learn, just not the most pleasant one.

The channeled material which follows may be relevant to all of us who are "too nice," who self-deprecate, and who become discouraged. The excerpts concern issues in Pete's personality and soul which were operative in his life. It also discusses my relationship with him over many lifetimes. I did not provide Pam any information about Pete's situation. Nor, to my knowledge, did she have any way of obtaining knowledge about my personal life. In fact, I did not even mention having a brother in the initial channeling. I simply called her up and said, "This is Joe. I want to know if I am doing all that I am supposed to be doing with my life."

June 1989

[This was my first session. It was held soon after Pete came to live at my office.]

Now with the dear man who I want to call Peter, who is in your life, you can give him great feelings of goodness and peace. He is your brother. In past lives there was a real hand-holding between you. There was a time when complete pleasure was impossible for him, as well as you. You did suffer much along the way with him. This sad man's childlike happy ways were lost for a very long time. On the road to bliss you did comfort him somewhat, gave over to him a stroke, a comfort, a ray of light—awakening him to what the happiness of play can do, to make a real man walk straight and proud in the world.

Now within himself, he self-deprecates much. And it is because of this that you have reached out a weary hand once more, to touch the controls of your dear brother's life—to bring him to the answers of childlike peace for which he does so struggle now, and seeks.

It is in essence a peculiar twist of fate that you happened on your brother's complexities at this time. For you have forgiven yourself little for some of your own. And so now it is in gaining, within, a presence of self-esteem, that you can come through your own fears about growing too powerful in your world.

August, 1989

[This next session occurred two months after my brother moved in with me and about two years before his suicide. My questions concerned options for Pete at this time, as I was disturbed by his depression and unemployment. I did not mention any concern of suicide. The channeler uses the word "they" to refer to ARGO, the nonphysical entity with whom she communicates.]

It is this kind of approach: "I will give back to myself what I gave to many others so that I will remember the pain of that." He is still consumed with so much guilt, and at this point so much self-deprecation that he can't feel that he could possibly deserve anything good in his life. He is to be the great giver and never to get a return on it.

So, that's the kind of thing that we are up against. He needs to see that it is his way of making amends. It is not the universe that says it must be this way. But there is just no way then to get a good job and manifest other good things when he is totally unable to see himself worthy of receiving anything and have any pride in his maleness nor pride in himself as a human light.

They were talking to me before you called about the need for you to lose a sense of responsibility about any decision of suicide, because you know in your profession that if someone decides something like this, there is really nothing one can do if they absolutely decide it. OK?

You've done your piece. They were showing the cord of light between Pete, the universe, and you—and it going as a triangle. They were cutting the cord between you and Pete. I think what they were talking about was the feeling of responsibility. But let's have them talk some more.

Dear child, you are indeed the window of relief for your dear son, Peter. See how it is in the window. Even now, he cannot get a clear view of a loving self. The window needs washing, not by your dear open hands, but by his own feelings of self-worth. The cleaning rag is already in his hands but he is too tired to rise to the windowsill to offer his first stroke. Self-will here is the determiner. The enjoyment he does feel now, of growing past the pain of physical life by giving self over to the order of things, is indeed what you are in vision of this day.

He does *not* wish to belong on the earth plane. However, the mild-manneredness of this dear child does not want death by violence. He has within him many components of fear, lashing out at self mostly about powerlessness, and also a great struggle, a will to survive this present crisis.

The opening at the other end of (they are showing me a corridor) now does lead him to brighter light, if he can accept that feeling good about life comes from believing in the living processes—that the enjoyment of sweet power comes from knowing who he is despite the angry retorts of the powerless who do surround him also.

He has been confronted by this kind of issue many times before and he cannot, even with anger about this, rush to the light with any feeling of capacity about how he is to gain entry in the doorway of loving. It is indeed a way of seeing self complete and whole that will end this tired man's anguish.

But you, within the circle of light, must hold on to the winner's circle. For you do feel in your own great integrity how your great power of mind and love have grown to show the world another order of things. And by remaining by your brother's death bed, you are reminded of how great the glory of light is, and how dark the narrow corridor of suffering is.

Grow more to show your sweet brother how the intensity of light gives off an ever-shining effervescence. And this can indeed be an example of how one lives when the will of God is allowed entry into one's soul. However, he is not presently equipped in his darkness to understand all of this.

Peter was your son many times before in past lives. And you did, in many ways, wish to teach him how to give great loving within a family, and how to be a great beacon of stability and honor. He sold the truth about this, though, during these times when he was your only son.

And you did not bend to his darkness but allowed his own trials and mistakes to address the currents of disbelief he held about loving. So, truly you were the winner of many matches during those currents of time when loving was shown between you.

Indeed, as you are holding his hand once more, you are not the brother so much as you are the father. And as you watch this dear suffering child lose a hold on his chance for re-birthing, the natural tendency of father's pride is to override the strict rules of give and take within the universal plane of light and to allow one final wash of cleansing love to give this dear child a chance to overcome what would be his last mistake.

As you rush to your brother's bedside to show him another washing light, he may consider the power of death greater than the power of light. For death gives him, as he sees it, a chance of accepting a droplet of loving from a Father far greater than anyone here on the earth plane. Through God the Father's eyes, he may, as indecent as he feels, see one shining chance at believing in loving.

He will instantly awaken from this dream state of earth-plane activity and ask to walk more directly on the proud roadway to heaven's loving gates. If you do see him becoming more despondent, give him a chance to talk with you about pride as a male. For if he feels power through this, he can answer his own unholy, anguished cries about being a demon who must be lost.

We are most blessed angels truly. We do walk through the winter months with your dear son, Peter. He has been so cold, yet he would not allow us to throw the great blanket of life around his bent shoulders. (They are showing me pictures of a child freezing, of them trying to comfort him with a blanket, and of him rejecting it. Then they show you coming in to try to do the same thing.) Realize that he is rejecting of light.

Certainly I feel no judgment on the other side about his decision, or panic about his decision. I really do not feel that. I feel more peace about this than I do about other things. I feel more compassion from them, as far as understanding the complete sense of loss he has—about who he is, as a soul. It goes so deep and, you know, I've heard them talk about other people who struggle but never with the same feeling that this man really has such a slim chance on this side, of hope.

He does have, as they say now, the window cleaner in his hand. He just doesn't have the strength to even begin it. I just don't feel this is all that imminent, possibly because he also is a very mild-mannered man and that he really doesn't like the idea of doing himself in. So that is an obstacle to it. It's the fatigue, it's the fatigue . . .

If he could feel what I feel on the other side for him, the gentle, compassionate, loving of him, he could possibly understand that he is loving. I guess I just wanted to translate to you the tenderness I feel from them—it's pretty powerful.

In the past lives you learned to let him take his lumps so that he could grow. But I think that as he took his lumps, he got angry and bitter and it just never worked well. But what I am hearing them say to you is that, as he has the opportunity to see you working as a light male, he at least has a vision of how that works and of the peace that it can bring. So he studies it. He also keeps you steady.

My dear son, the working is so hard to do now, that this dear child simply cannot believe himself holy enough to pull himself up by the bootstraps and take life on as a quest of joy. The amount of drainage is so great and his faculties so low for understanding, that neither the brother, nor the father, nor the sister, nor the mother could call him from where he sits. His ego is in displacement now.

The power of light is extraordinary surrounding him. As you have been about the place where he lives cleansing and powdering it, you have created indeed a holy castle.

A long-term effect of brain damage also is a part of your dear brother's problem. There lies within him a . . . (They are showing me pictures now. They are showing a graying area in the brain—small, not a big deal).

This does not show as a powerful problem in this dear child's life. But it allows some erratic emotional responses to take place. Accordingly, he is not able to respond as positively as you would wish. So please be certain also of this behavior pattern, as it was a current growing through his life from early childhood. They are just showing a very, very sensitive little boy. Worrying easily about things, and then responding. And it is part of the current problem.

When he goes to relate with anyone (and they are showing from work into personal relationships) there is a piece of him that can't accurately read what is given to him. And because he can't read it, he will frequently withdraw and be very nice, so that things can be smooth, and he won't get into an interaction that seems to him to be out of control.

Instead of sympathizing so much, listen with another ear and then run through with him what might really be happening. Although he feels very betrayed by many people, he has brought a lot of this on himself. Sometimes he asks something of them, misinterprets the response, and then reacts to that. So he makes himself a victim, where sometimes he wasn't. On a psychological level, that is what is going on with him now. On a spiritual level, it is the other piece that we have been talking about.

You and your dear wife struggle to hand self-worth to this dear child. Please know that as you work with him in such an intense fashion, you are really getting a one-sided story when he tells you what has happened to him. Give him loving support always with a clear-eyed vision that you believe in his power.

Now they show a picture of the two of you walking down a roadway and for you to let his hand go. And I think that means as far as the responsibility for keeping him here.

Much of the information conveyed in these first two channelings seemed true to me at some deep level. It felt very strange to hear it. The material about past-life interactions with Pete felt like a dream you can almost remember, that calls to you to remember.

My wife and I had indeed been trying to shower him with love, encouragement, and playfulness since he had come to live with us. The parts of the channeling that spoke of his feelings of lack of self-worth resonated with our understanding of him. I wept as I heard how tired he was and that I needed to let go. But I put that part behind me as fast as I could and defiantly renewed my efforts to help him. Two months later, we had another session, followed by occasional sessions in the two years that followed.

October 1989

Now, it doesn't look good for Pete job-wise almost anywhere until he works through these issues. As he continues to put himself out there, he is going to become more depressed because of the same blocked doorways.

Dear child, it would be most important for you to know that although your dear son, Peter, does indeed live in great respect for the spiritual mind, he does create the limit of what he can expect for himself, when he is contained in a physical form. (While Pete believes in the goodness of the soul, he doubts the goodness of man on Earth.)

Please let him know that he does transfer great light within self when he does enjoy his excursions into the paranormal (out-of-body experiences). *Please know that man is equipped with light, that man is given the boundaries of his own physical world only because he chooses to understand limit.* As Peter and you become limitless in your excursions out-of-body, please do also know that man is of great light, that man is of great love, that man can be carried in his fullest expression, to the outer boundaries of joyous receptivity.

The theme that they are showing me is that somewhere in Pete's belief system there is a split between the power of light and the beauty of human, and that, as these are separated, it separates man from receiving his light.

February 1990

The way your sweet brother Peter does work through his rejection is an example for you. Realize how that kind of belief in karmic destiny does make a man impotent. It is important, however, for you to realize also that some of these suicidal tendencies came from an early chemical imbalance. There is a history of this within your entire family, not just within you or your brother.

Be brave, my son; the work with the chemical imbalance within yourself is almost completed. It is because you were interacting more proudly and willingly with the male energy that you were able to light the fires of a more exacting hormonal base than was he.

June 1990

[Pete requested before he went out to Las Vegas that I ask in this session whether the Vegas area would be good for him.]

OK, I'm trying to get a little clearer because they are showing a cyclone around him. Just a cyclone. Oh boy, they just show him being blown with the cyclone.

Charge Pete more completely with the feelings of being responsible for himself. And release yourself also from personal responsibility of him. Now coming up your way is a breach of contract. Realize that, at times, in your overcommitment to heal others, you fail to grant to them their own freedom to choose. So it would be again that in the letting go, you arrive at God's love.

I feel that the breach of contract is more of a friend letting you down. I think it's somebody that you believe you would help and then they fall apart. I would suspect that it is Pete, but I do not know that. And that's where you are really going to learn to let go. It is someone you've poured a tremendous amount of energy into, who chooses differently.

The dear child, Pete, does not have the desire intensely enough to heal self—to release the unworthiness he feels in his heart. He has at this time broken with the commitment, however, to die. So we do not see yet a departure from the earth plane. But the unkindness this dear man had shown toward others in past lives does still haunt the inner beings of his soul.

He must know that as he works his way westward, hard times would be coming. He is a man without a center of grounding, or knowing where his home lies, and the turmoil of a city like Las Vegas leaves him feeling much more the same.

He is now seeing most of man as gross. Without the details of living securely on this earth plane, he is consumed by fright of defeat. Tell him to watch out for addictive behavior, as it could be aggravated in such a place. However, desire on his part to move ahead is being honored by all of us. As you do know, we are eager angels of love waiting to hear his call of friendship and light.

By understanding more how this child is power-driven to destruction, you may leave him alone to his journey of choices, and know that your love does go with him. He will live a singular life for a while. He is trying. But he is not out of the cyclone yet.

July 3 1991
[This session occurred about ten days before Pete died.]

Now, allowing (I think this must be Pete they are talking about) others to travel on their own way right now is most important. This man has decided to become self-taught and must learn the lesson of letting go of all judgment. (They show him out in the desert; is he still out around Nevada?)

As he is a man walking through the desert, he has the time now to take off the old clothing, to view the nakedness of his true self, and learn how to draw his own succulence from the dry desert sand. He is not as afraid to receive his succulence as he once was. Because of that, he feels that he can ask of himself much forgiveness now. And on his own, he can complete much of the self-healing work that was attempted on your glorious farmland.

Set him free and, as you feel the warm brotherliness next to him, see how you responded to your own lack of self-respect in a very different way. He chose to torment himself, through lack of forgiveness, for being powerless. You used it to challenge others to find their light.

I feel really good about Pete [First time you have said that.] Yes, it is and I am thrilled! There is hope in him. They are showing this tunnel of light piercing through some very dark funnel clouds. He can see the light there. The path is crooked, but I really think Pete will make it to a place where he is comfortable about who he is, where he can say "OK, I've landed now."

This was the last channeling concerning Pete before his death. There were many sessions after his death, and those were a source of understanding and comfort for me. They led me to consider possibilities and hinted at the reasons why I felt such an intense connection with him beyond what I knew consciously. We'll return to those sessions later.

In the only channeling Pete had directly, he reported that he received information that in a past life he had been a powerful king who had been fair but not merciful. Many people were severely punished at his hand to keep order and safety in his realm. This fit what I knew of him. While I have literally seen him give the shirt off his back to a person in need—as well as his last five dollars—he also believed that those who repeatedly or severely hurt others should be shot.

The channeling stated that he now felt the need to pay back this debt and to stay far away from power. They suggested that Pete imagine himself going down a flight of stairs to a doorway and see himself opening the door and viewing a king counting his money inside of the room. In the exercise, Pete was to forgive the king and release him and all karma from that lifetime.

ARGO suggested to him that the way of karma (cause leading to effect) is a slow and hard way to learn the route back to the Light. The Law of Love, however, allows instant redemption and is available to us all at any time. Love surrounds us in any plane of existence we may inhabit. Yet free will is at all times respected, even our choice to turn away from the Light. But love will fulfill its intent to include and embrace all in the end.

The perspective gained from Pam's channeled information provided some comfort during those last years with Pete, and also after his death. But after he was gone, there were great oceans of grief to swim through.

MY BODY CARRIES ME FOR NOTHING[19]
August 15, 1991

My body carries me for nothing
Like the ocean carries logs.
Pain in my brother's body
Exacted a constant price.

My mind holds possibilities
Innumerable.
Brother's mind held hopelessness
Immeasurable.

My heart contained joy—
The affirmation of others.
My brother's was broken—
Too torn to vessel.

My heart now is leaking.
I hope his is free.

Our genes roughly sang
The same song.
In essential ways
None were closer

Two me
Now one me
Alone.

He's gone.
I'm sort of here.
That's the current "isness."

I may learn how
To follow this Tao.
Sad log on this ocean
I don't have to like it.

5 ∞ DAMAGE CONTROL

The first months after my brother's death, much of my focus was a form of damage control—taking care of others and struggling to function myself. I went back to visit my mom and dad, fearing what I would find. We sat on their screen porch for several cool Berkshire summer evenings, listening to the wind in the pines and the crickets chirping. We talked. They were indeed deeply wounded, still in shock. Staying in shock could be fatal. And if they came out of it, the impact might also kill them.

Despite his unhappiness, Pete had always looked terrific in our parents' presence. He was ruggedly handsome. I had always thought that he looked and carried himself a lot like James Garner in *Maverick*. Pete wore his soft, dark brown, wavy hair combed back on both sides with no part. He never changed this style, and his hair was never mussed. His bright blue eyes carried a mischievous sparkle that was softened by his friendly smile and suggested a playful intelligence. He kept himself fit, tan, and trim. His clothes were always clean, neat, and of good quality. He had an amazing body grace. In short, whenever he was around my parents he looked like a million bucks in a happy and gentle way.

My mother talked openly during my visit about her son Peter, the man she remembered as so handsome and fit. She would try to stop the conversations before crying, but she was only partially successful. The talks tended to be short, with her beginning again an hour or two later, after regaining some composure. Mom couldn't believe it; couldn't believe that the precious infant she had held at her breast was gone, that the bright, eager, and helpful boy she had taken so much pride in was gone, that the strong, kind man with whom she had spent the wee hours of the morning talking was gone. He was her shining jewel. She had spent her life, like most mothers, worrying often about all the things that could happen to her children. Yet never had it crossed her mind to prepare for this.

Mom knew that somehow this was her fault. She politely listened otherwise but secretly repeated the chant: "How did I fail him? It must have been something I didn't give him, my most beloved son. Oh God! It cannot be true that he is gone." In her desolation, nearly eighty years of devout Catholicism offered no comfort. The Catholic training also set her up for dreading that her lovely son was in hell for eternity, for the Church had taught her early in life that suicide was a mortal sin. She struggled. Faith equalled terror. Rejection of faith meant the possibility that he was at peace but that there may be no God.

My dad deflected most inquiries about how he was doing or what he was experiencing with brief answers. He went daily to Pete's grave site to tend the flowers. He was fairly even on the surface. I think he was also the first one to feel any anger. I think his anger came from Pete wasting the precious gift of life and from seeing how grievously his suicide was hurting others. When he thought he was in private, we heard my dad at times sobbing deeply. That was harder to bear than my mother's tears because it was difficult to know how to try to console him without invading his privacy. I did go in once to hold him and he accepted it for a few moments.

I looked to my parents as models of how to deal with my own feelings. But neither parent's approach seemed right for me at the time, although both were to be admired for coping at all. Strangely, a blend of their styles seemed right for me, a blend of grief and going on with daily life.

On the plane back home from this visit, I became aware that my relationship with Pete as I had known it had ceased to exist. To find him again in spirit, I had to throw previous conceptions away and search for a transformed Peter and perhaps a new me.

This newness felt true in my relationship to my parents also. Lost were our old roles. We were now marked by a common wound that no longer allowed the illusion of a big strong parent and a responsibility-free child. Yet it was obvious that we valued each other even more than before. I wanted a new relationship with them—an intimacy that had room to grow even through the veil of eventual death. I jotted this poem down as the plane floated me home.

My father is a gentleman.
My mother a sad angel.
Well, they have lit my way.

As I open my heart to them
Tonight
A radiance warms my chest.

It is joy to treasure them
And know they love me.
But now we grow further.

One last shell to crack
Before we go clear
Into deeper intimacy.

It is time to stop "sonning"
And fathering and mothering.
We release, to meet again as equals.

To see each other, truly
We release forty-year patterns
And find eternity.

This direction felt like the right one for me with these two dear people. I was so glad that they had each other. In their fifty-five years of marriage they had created many ways to know and convey their regard for each other. Love is often a celebration. Now it would be their anchor.

On the other side of things, I still was a parent of a young child. And my child needed me to stay in the father role for a good while longer. The hardest thing was that I could not promise what she felt that she needed the most—for me never to go away from her. Seven-year-olds let themselves clearly feel the distinction between "most probably" and "yes."

My daughter was devastated. Pete had been her loving companion. I remember him holding her tenderly for hours when she was a baby. Later he teased her gently in a way that made her feel big and proud. He would delight her with tricks such as putting cigarettes in each of his nostrils and ears and acting as if nothing was unusual no matter how much she reacted. After he was living with us, he would take her for a full day's adventure and bring her back smiling and safe.

Now she was worried that everyone would die. She didn't want to go to school, or on field trips to the zoo, or anywhere out of our sight. The nausea she had experienced during the funeral continued. Fearing she would get sick, she carried an airsickness bag wherever she went. She began wetting the bed.

Her questions were constant and often upset the fragile equilibrium her parents were attempting to maintain. Unexpectedly she would ask the hard questions. Was the undertaker sad when he picked up Pete's body? How come Pete was depressed? Why couldn't the doctors help him? Do you feel it when you are cremated? Why do people have funerals, if it makes everyone so sad? Is it allowed to kill yourself?

While we gathered blueberries, she would ask, "Who found Pete?"

While we were folding laundry, she would be talking about school and suddenly say, "How did Pete hold the gun?"

As I was putting her to bed, finally thinking I had her peaceful and settled, she would look me directly in the eye and ask, "Wasn't Pete scared?"

On and on.

Yet my daughter also stated firmly that if Pete wanted peace, it was his decision. She insisted that Pete came and talked to her the night we heard the news and also on the plane going up to the funeral. She said he spoke clearly, talking inside her head and telling her that it would be all right, that he was fine, that her Mommy and Daddy would stop being sad after a while.

Pete's son had just graduated with a master's degree a week or so before his father's suicide. I suspect that Peter had waited until he discharged all the responsibilities that he could toward his son. Pete had often talked with a warm pride about the chance at a good life that his son would have. But his son was blind-sided by the suicide. You could see him falter within the pseudo-sureness of young adulthood. A very private person by nature, he was now caught between loyalty to his dad and confusion at the ugliness revealed.

I cared powerfully for my family and they for me. I found myself being so grateful for them and proud of how all were striving to do the best that they could under the burden of grief. There was no trace of pettiness (Whom did he love best?), no hint of nervous, macabre humor—only dignity, suffering, and compassion.

Toward the end of the first month, I was beginning to understand the magnitude of my personal loss. He had become my best friend in the two years he lived with me. I began remembering all he did for me as a child. He used to let me hit him as hard as I could in his rock-hard stomach. He never budged or grunted, yet each year he said I was getting stronger. I would tell him to hit me back, but he never did so with humiliating force.

He tried repeatedly to get me to learn how to shoot a gun for protection. I always declined because I feared violence. Finally, after I had a daughter to protect, I let him show me how to use a pistol. The lesson was short. On a bright summer's day he carefully went over the rules and safety procedures and then aimed at a tree about thirty feet away in our front yard. The bullet buried deep, right on the mark. He gave me the gun. I fired and then swept the still-loaded pistol right past him as I gestured at something. He quickly paled, stepping backward in surprise, said, "Maybe you'd better leave guns alone," and took back his pistol. I agreed. I think that was the gun he used to leave us.

I dreamt of him about three weeks after his death. In the dream, I was trying to put a window screen on a window. No matter what I did, it would not fit. Pete came up gently behind, put his hands on mine, and guided the screen to a perfect fit. I turned and asked him if he could now talk about what he had done. He turned his face away sadly and said, "No." Then he faded away.

I began to know the hope and dread of mourners—to encounter their lost loved ones in their dreams. Here contact was completely real, an incredible sense that he was here in the flesh. Then I would wake, realize I was "only dreaming," and experience the freshness of the wound all over again.

It was so difficult to express what was going on. Hell, it was hard to even feel it, let alone try to share it with others. The sense of isolation was acute. My clients were very caring of me in the weeks after I got back from the funeral. But they had their own pain, and I was supposed to be helping them. I found that I had zero patience for pettiness, trivia, or issues of vengefulness or violence. It took all I could do to sit there and not explode when these human feelings surfaced in my clients. But it was even worse when my clients or friends had some sorrow to express. Then I would be overwhelmed with grief at all the pain in the world. All of a sudden, it seemed like everyone was grieving somebody or something.

In my two decades of clinical work, I had counseled many who had lost loved ones. From this work I knew that although they usually kept the incidents private, many experienced contact with their departed. The typical pattern of contact was a fleeting sense of presence within the first hours or days after the death, then months of no contact, and finally, if they were lucky, a re-establishment of connection that would be felt at unpredictable times. I now tried to meditate and use Lifeline and other techniques to reach Pete myself. My desire for contact was powerful, but I felt no clear response, no real sense of him. Knowing the usual pattern of contact did not console me.

I began to fear that I was unworthy and would never be skilled enough, and even that the reports of such connection were all nonsense.

I stopped watching television—couldn't take the news reports of the inhumanity of man, the triviality of sitcoms, or the constant commercials for unneeded products. In self-defense, I dove into numerous projects. I had a novel, three professional articles, and several seminars all going at the same time. My personal energy has always been high. Now it was becoming hard to just get up and get breakfast, but, once I was going, it was hard to stop. I have never been through anything so draining in my life.

About a month after Pete died, I realized that I had yet to spend a day fully alone with myself and my feelings. I scheduled it in. It began with me waking up at 4:00 A.M., unable to sleep. I opened a book someone had given me about surviving a loss by suicide. I read it from cover to cover, finishing by 7:00 A.M., and found myself furious. The book was filled with platitudes and trite observations, or at least it seemed so at the time.

I spent the day raging around the house—defeated, depressed, and confused. This wasn't the neat and clean grief that I had always read about in which you feel sad, cry, and then feel better. There was no sense of contact with Pete, no felt comfort from God, no sense of closure. So much for getting in touch with one's feelings! After that day I went back to being overly busy, and took my grief in small hard chunks that, while they burned terribly, at least didn't choke me going down.

A different variety of experience was also building within me, as I came out of the initial shock. My grieving seemed to be feeding a part of my soul. I would be caught by the beauty of the most ordinary objects, and become absorbed and transported by the exquisite loveliness of small things in nature, even rocks and pebbles. I think that I was moving so often to thoughts of my brother and the world of the physically dead, searching so much for him in the beyond, that I had loosened my moorings to the physical world. This separation allowed me fresh appreciation of the magnificence of our physical world each time I re-entered it from my thoughts of faraway.

Through my experience of beauty and more often through pain, I was acutely aware that I was alive. The pain gradually changed. Somewhere in the second week, I went a day without crying. Somewhere in the second month I went a day without thinking of my brother. There was an emerging commitment to live my own life more fully. The pledge involved being more honest with myself and with others about who I was and what I wanted.

While it was part of being fully alive, I found it was not easy for me to be honest about all that I really wanted. It brought up fears that I might not fulfill my dreams, that I might lose other things I valued in the trying, and that maybe I was being selfish. By facing these fears, it became possible to discover that life can be a win-win situation and to know that pursuit of happiness is indeed a birthright. Such pursuit needs to be balanced with responsibility, not weakened by fears of hurting self or others. It can be a dynamic balance between vigorous self-fulfillment and vital brotherhood.

All this was a quiet counterpoint to the dragging upward from shock and loss. I mention it here because these issues of aliveness and soul are, I suspect, part of the core nature of the grieving process as much as the tears are. Deep grieving changes us forever. It is different from the small unsettlement we experience when we hear of strangers' deaths, different even from the genuine sadness and uneasiness that the death of someone closer produces. In these situations we eventually go back to pretty much who we were before. But the death of a parent, sibling, or one of our children is not dismissed so easily. It transforms us—breaking us apart. We put ourselves back together in a new way or not at all.

Suicide highlights how much choice we have as human beings and how little of that awesome freedom we usually use in our daily lives. We have near-total freedom of attitude, freedom of how we treat ourselves and others, freedom of what to focus upon, freedom to coast, tear down, or build up.

Suicide also highlights our power as human beings. When we see the death of another affect so many people we love in such radical ways, we are brought to an undeniable awareness that each person has a profound influence on the well-being of others. When we drop the stones of our actions into the waters of the Earth community, the circles cross the planet and echo far into future time. This is a power that we often like to deny. I began wondering how many of my stones were jewels and how many were millstones.

When we become aware of both our freedom and power within the precious days of physical life, it is hard not to feel that we've been lazy, stingy, or cowardly in our use of such gifts. We feel an urgency to finally live up to our potential, before our ending. Suicide shines as a lighthouse beacon, warning of unmet potential, false perceptions, and life-denying self-deprecation—too late to correct. To the extent we are guilty of these same crimes, suicide makes us uneasy.

Life also demands surrender—letting go of fears and attachments. To live well we must die each day to what is no longer useful, living, and vital in our lives. Releasing necrotic thoughts and behaviors allows rebirth each morning to the infinity of possibilities. Few people practice and are good at these mini-deaths. My brother surrendered his life with a gunshot rather than surrendering his deadening thoughts and behaviors. How many more of us slowly and quietly lose what makes us feel most alive, rather than give up an attitude or behavior that is no longer productive?

We like to call it a rut we fall into. It is really more accurately described as a grave. So, I had to learn how to surrender my brother. Maybe after I could do this, letting go of all that is dead in me would be possible for the first time.

I keep a personal journal sporadically. In the weeks after Pete's death, I recorded my observations and opinions, and also reports from family members concerning their feelings of connection with Pete after his passing. Here are some samples of what we were experiencing.

My Own Experience:
[These are excerpts from my journal in the period immediately following Pete's death.]

Pete died yesterday. I felt great agitation after hearing the news until, at Teena's suggestion, I lay down for a half-hour at 3:00 P.M. today and attempted to calm myself and open to Pete. I felt an immediate sense of lightness and well-being that carried into the rest of the day including the flight to Massachusetts and meeting my family. The lightness was different in quality than ever experienced before. It was subtle yet powerful, and allowed feelings of joy at the beauty of clouds and sunset. The lightness seemed to bathe me both from above and from within.

* * *

Through great agitation in the few days after Pete's death, until after the funeral, whenever I made time to lie down and relax, this same feeling of lightness was present and lasted for a few hours each time. At the funeral, though I was very sad, I felt supported by good energy. I was able to read Pete's eulogy in a strong and calm voice.

It was strange to see a white 1962 T-Bird convertible outside the back of the church when we exited from the funeral—best of my recollection, it was Pete's favorite car. [I have not seen that car, before or since, in that small town of three thousand people. The next time I was there I asked about town and could find no one who knew who owned the car.]

* * *

After the tree planting, when I meditated, I felt a very strong wave of gratitude toward me. It didn't feel directly like Pete (none of his personality seemed present). I had the feeling then that I was looking for the old Pete, that now he was transformed to an extent that his energy was much lighter and more delicate, happier, cleaner.

* * *

We have returned home after the funeral. When we got

home to North Carolina from the funeral, our new BMW started immediately at the airport. The next morning the truck battery was dead. I went to start the lawn mower—the 2-month-old battery was also dead and had a hole in the top with acid bubbling out. The next morning my electric razor battery was dead and would not recharge.

We went to the office. My wife heard noises upstairs (where Pete had lived) in the evening when she was alone in the building. She went to leave and found that the BMW's battery was dead. The next morning we checked the upstairs of the office. The room used by a massage therapist was locked from the inside. It had never been locked before, and we had to hunt to find a key. That night, when we returned home, the garage door opener battery was dead.

Was Pete signalling us through all the dead batteries, or was he pulling energy for his own use? Were we pulling energy for our own use? Was it just a series of coincidences? Strange that so much of this had to do with cars, which were one of Pete's favorite things.

My Wife's Experience:

My wife too wondered at the battery experiences. Additionally, she meditated at the same time I did on the day after Pete died, and had the same feeling of lightness afterwards, despite great agitation beforehand; the lightness extended the same amount of time as mine.

My Daughter's Experience:

After being home a few days after the funeral, my daughter volunteered that when I had told her the news of Pete's death and we were crying together, she had heard Pete's voice saying "It is going to be all right." The morning after his death, she seemed very calm when she woke up, and she told me that if Pete had called her before he died and told her what he was going to do, she would not have tried to stop him—that it was his choice.

Then on the plane to the funeral in Massachusetts she heard him again, saying to her, "I love you—don't be afraid." She heard him again another time when she closed her eyes and felt that she could talk to him easily.

At the family gathering she was exceptionally good, positive, undemanding, and helpful. She seemed agitated only at contemplating the funeral and then during the funeral. She says she misses him often but seems to feel still connected somehow. When she talks with a friend, it is with a great deal of acceptance about what has happened. In my clinical experience this is unusual for a six-year-old.

My Brother John's Experience:

On the morning after Pete's death, before he had heard the news, John woke up to find blood on his pillow and no injury on his body that could account for it. Pete had shot himself in the head on his bed in Las Vegas only hours before.

The Sunday after Pete's death, while in church, John experienced a strong wave of energy that felt as if it would push him right out of the back of the church. At this time he heard the words "He is with me." These words seemed to come directly from God. The words were accompanied by a profound sense of consolation that lasted at least into the next few days. John is aware of no psychic experiences in his life before then.

Pete's Girlfriend's Experience:

She reports many small things, such as complete strangers coming up to her and starting to talk about things that are unusual for people to talk about yet seemed consoling and relevant to her grieving process. She reports feeling Pete's presence strongly much of the time, so much so that she is having trouble being focused on the physical plane.

Three days after Pete's death, I contacted Pam Hogan, the channeler. Here are notes from that session.

Pam was reluctant to focus on Pete's transition, as often she feels the person's agitation and physical experience at the time of death, when she attempts to focus so soon after transition.

Through ARGO, Pam was fed the following information: That the final straw for Pete was fear of abandonment and aloneness with respect to an exclusive adult partnering relationship. That his connections with family were well and good but he needed more. That energies set up from long past pulled him to a choice of repeating old patterns even more intensely. He felt he had to break out of those patterns somehow.

His need to borrow so much money, and a deep sense of indebtedness and hopelessness about changing this, also weighed on Pete heavily. There was nothing anyone could have done to help at this point.

After a short initial period of scattered energy right after his death, she felt Pete settling down quickly, so that by 5:00 P.M. yesterday she saw him as jubilant, tucked in, resting, and very glad to be home. He has a feeling of being in a very child-like, trusting, sleep—finally having a deep feeling of safety about himself and where he is now. ARGO protects Pam from lowered or erratic vibrations. It may be appropriate to directly channel Pete later, but not now. Pete's vibration now might drain her some.

The deeds Peter did were chosen over a lifetime. He negated much of the good that may have come to him. He has been taken now to a resting post by a legion of angels to dissipate his weariness, so he can come to understand that he does have endurance. His aloneness was most painful to him.

He wants to contact you, Joe. He wants to plant seeds in your mind. He wants to work hard with you to effect some changes. He will be on the observation plane for a while. Maintain a very high, light energy level. He will observe the high vibration of your examples. A while from now, his own light will glow more magnificently and can reach your light more easily, after his vibrations smooth and raise up. Communication can occur more easily later, in a more relaxed manner later, after he has rested.

[I asked if there was anything we could do to help him now].

Send thoughts of celebration at the new birthing of Peter. Send thoughts of death as warmth. Both these thoughts will add warmth to his resting sleep. Also, live your own life in a way that reflects "coming into your own light and power." This will help teach him how things can go. Delay strong attempts at two-way communication a few months—he is a weary man. It will be much easier to hear him later. Look for him on the observation plane. This is above the astral plane. They show him later with a notebook, taking notes and learning rapidly, learning by observing things on the physical plane: For example, "Oh, when a person does this, that is the result."

It is significant that I felt so alone and lost, even with these early feelings of contact in myself, in my family, and through Pam. These things were a paltry substitute for having Pete right next to me alive, visible, and tangible.

A MONTH OF YEARS
August 30, 1991

It has been a month of years
Since my brother's suicide.

I can't find love hymns written for brothers.
Perhaps it's too sacred to sing about easily.

But, then again—I find little song
To connect with now.

Moments of sad love drift by.
I cling to the debris—it quickly melts.

Mother frail, held her son weeping.
Now ugly dawn reveals crucifixion.
Hoping for Resurrection yet unable to pray.

Father strong and proud in his loving.
I heard the hurricane crack the oak.
Are we now in the eye?

Young son launching outward
Forced to return by the currents of sorrow
In the air and the water.

Sister inscrutable.
Another burden to carry on her bent shoulders
Through darkness plodding.

One brother wondering.
Fears the power of negative thinking
And his own hard circumstances.

One brother quiet yet ready to smash things.
A blanket of emptiness,
A pillow of guilt.

Myself in frustration
No light felt.
Where are the angels?

Gentlest of spirits, lover assaulted.
Having to harden against multiple losses.

Wife or Ex-wife—is there really a difference?
Does divorce soften widowhood, or remove support?

The left-behinds have felt all the feelings
Each is holding in this symphony of grief.

Friends, acquaintances, landlords, bank-tellers
All stop to pause troubled, missing a piece.

The circles widen, lapping the lives
Of all who know his fine family.

Each and all torn
By an isolated man
Who tried to leave neatly.

From his point of view
It was a act of hard love.

A mystery of surrender—
We must surrender to.

6 ∞ SUPPORT

Before encountering the blessed burden of our freedom, we meet our own helplessness. When we are children, adults make and enforce unwanted decisions. Later, we can't make certain people like us, turn back our biological clocks, or undo some of our actions. One of the hardest limitations to live with is seeing a person we love suffering, when we can't seem to do anything to help. The agony we feel when we are powerless to help is one of the most beautiful things about human beings. We are not indifferent creatures.

Men and women both feel this helplessness acutely. But men may be more shamed by it. Men are taught to act upon the world, to protect, and to accomplish tangible results. Sometimes for men the ability to create a result is more important than whether the result is good or bad!

This chapter explores my powerlessness, after my brother's passing, to help my wife Charleene with her grief. My life partner-lover is also a clinical psychologist and is an excellent therapist. She, like I, was acquainted with mourning from the intellectual side—psychological theories of grieving. She was also familiar with the role of supporter of others, as they worked through their misfortunes in therapy. But the loss of Pete still overwhelmed her. Massive in itself, his death occurred amidst a series of losses for Charleene.

Not long before Pete's death, after three years of effort to adopt a child, we were offered a chance to adopt a boy, due to be born within the month. After he was born, we told everyone, named him, set up the nursery with stuffed bears and a crib, and awaited his arrival in our home. Charleene was just beaming—happier than I had ever seen her. Days passed, then weeks. The mother changed her mind and kept "our" son. This loss hit us as strongly as would the miscarriage of a passionately desired child. Soon after, my wife had to have a hysterectomy, ruling out biological children forever. Then her dog died, after being her faithful pet for fifteen years. Two of our cats died. Charleene's best friend moved to Missouri. The winter before Peter's suicide, her grandfather passed away.

Our daughter fell off a roof and cracked her hip three weeks before Pete died. Her head had just missed a sharp-edged concrete barrel and we had quite a scare. Two weeks later, Charleene's car was totalled. She was all right physically but shaken again.

On the day of Pete's funeral, my wife received the news that her eighty-five-year-old grandmother, two thousand miles away, was undergoing emergency surgery to have the valves replaced in her heart. My wife stayed with me and our daughter for Pete's funeral and hoped for the best. Her losses continued; her grandmother, a wonderful woman, followed her husband of sixty-two years into death within two years of his passing.

One of the hardest things about my brother's death time was watching my wife suffer—to see her normal cheerfulness, gracefulness, and extroversion withering. She had met Pete with a totally open heart. They had become very close. He became the loving brother she had always wanted. They would work in the kitchen together, chatting and laughing. He would watch her practicing karate, always praising her progress yet honoring her femininity. Even though she had feared that suicide was a possibility for Pete, she had been unable to defend herself. She still slammed full force into the wall of pain.

Now her rock and protector—I—was self-absorbed and removed from her. I could still say the right things occasionally, but my spirit was somewhere far away much of the time. I was struggling with my own demons as she was with hers. It was different than being absent due to having an affair; I had a right to pull energy away from the marriage for this and in fact had no choice. But our contract stated, "When I need you the most, you will be there." This time I wasn't there—not fully.

She knew that my own bouts of depression were sometimes severe in the past. She wondered how much pull I would feel to join my brother in death. She had thought that I would never abandon her that way. Yet I was absent right now—something that was inconceivable before. It was a scary time for her, adding fear to her own grief and efforts to care for our daughter and my family. But I was unable to share much about myself. Instead, we talked about how to help our daughter and others through this time. And Charleene and I connected most through simple things—enjoying the good taste of food, holding hands, our goodnight kiss and snuggle. There is a lot of power in simple things.

Some men rage, but most are silent when feeling impotence of any kind. I was silently furious at my helplessness during much of this time. Men, when silent, usually need understand- ing—building up of self-concept and empowerment once again. Men look automatically to women for fulfillment of this need, although they will seldom request support directly. But at the time of my brother's death, a woman's support was not what I was seeking. I needed something different. I needed male support but had little experience in obtaining it. It was almost taboo.

Historically, men have tended to be suspicious and compet- itive with other men, feeling they cannot afford to lose face. Fortunately, this is gradually changing. In the awkward drum- ming of men's groups, issues with non-nurturing fathers and the absence of mentors are being explored. This is good both because women are already overburdened by men's neediness and because the only place for men to get certain things of value may be from other men. Men can teach each other to thrive, and to powerfully husband their families and the Earth once again.

Feeling the loss of my brother's friendship and mentoring, I started a men's group in the fall of the year of my brother's passing. It was less scary than joining a group of strangers who might drum, cry, or hug without warning. As a leader, I had some control. But it was still uncomfortable. We sat facing each other in early sessions nervously glancing at the speaker who usually was talking to the ceiling. Later, we could joke that it was okay to cry but "Don't try to hug me!" Eventually, finally, embracing each other in sorrow and in joy felt natural and right.

Gradually I learned to let go of tight control and became more of a participant than a leader. The group was invaluable to me in dealing with the issues of grieving, vulnerability, and fear. It was a major factor in my coming to know and trust the frank strength and nurturing of men. This is one gift of my brother's life and death.

My loss of my brother shattered my sense of value and power. My old sense of these things was based mostly on my ability to perform. The role of provider, protector, gardener, listener, and friend were important to me. I did them well because I loved those roles and am blessed with a talent for them. I still perform these functions well but am adding new roles that are in some ways more expansive, such as teacher, writer, gambler, and playmate.

My new, re-built sense of power and value is anchored more deeply. It is anchored in my being as a male and as a person. I still honor my therapist healing skill as a valuable and potent gift. However, all illusions of invincibility have vanished; I understand that I cannot guide the course of events where another person's free will is present, regardless of the strength of my intent.

The men's group and many friendships with both women and men are helping me recover. But by far and away, the strength of my marriage and my wife's fineness of person has been both my reason to try and my main well of healing. And I am finally able to support her once again.

We often think, "Boy I've got to do everything myself." But it is good to remember that if we seek support, we can find another human who will try hard to help us with the big questions, sorrows, and burdens that surface in our lives. That person is often as close as the next room, or the phone. We should celebrate that there are always people who will help us carry our weight of power, or helplessness—if we let them know that we are hurting.

THE HIGH QUEEN CRIES
August 30, 1991

What's to be done?
The high queen cries
But has to go on.

Noble heart healer
Lightest of spirits
Now dimmed by sorrow.

I stand by, her king,
As wounds drop from the sky.
My impotence galls me.

First her grandfather
Captured by cancer.
Next her own womb is taken.

Her daughter, falling
Slips from her arms
Hitting cruel pavement.

Her best friend is leaving
Will be far way.
What else can happen?
Why on this day?

Her car crashes.
Belts burn her skin.
Her substitute brother
Does himself in.

I, her husband,
Pull back into grief.
No one to hold her,
Little relief.

This woman I love
Is carrying too much.
Will no angel help her
Till I can re-touch?

Both in exhaustion,
Yet love holds us.
Our bond is for life.
It pierces through death.

Can I remind her:
Of magic snow kisses
Under moonlit pines?
Of laughter till tears run
That are not bitter?

Of communion of mind,
Moon to her star?
Of body delight.
Refreshment and grace?

Of building home beauty,
A haven for the small?
Of creating our work,
Compassion for all?

Two decades young
Our love now is fire.
The tempering of steel
The purpose of pyre.

I'll stay with her always
I'll pierce any veil,
Whether fortune plays lightly
Or nails us below.
I love my bride deeply,
Help her please, know.

7 ∞ ECHOES

By the early fall of the year, three months after Pete died, our daily weeping had stopped, except for my mother's. And by then, even she had good moments during her days. For each member of my family, some semblance of normality returned. As Charleene and I harvested grapes and made a rich, clear juice that captured sunshine for the winter, we could smile and feel our link with the Earth. Yet much grief work continued.

Thank God, my daughter could now be caught singing and skipping once again. She was still anxious about separation in the mornings before school and in the evenings at bedtime, but her questions were now fewer. And I could respond to her with less distress.

Her queries usually came while we were driving in the car or working in the garden. One short question, then on to something else, usually after the statement "I miss Pete" and my resonance, "I know honey, so do I."

She remained interested in the mechanics and technology of death: How hot was a cremation fire? Did I want to be cremated? Her questions concerning how someone is chosen for death contained a singular tension: When would I die? When would she die? As she picked up the understanding that the best predictor was age, it became "How old is" every pet and person she knew. She would comment on how hard it would be if they died and how much she would miss them. She figured that her great-grandma was next in line, and she was right—but not for a while yet.

My daughter was adopted at birth. Now her questions turned to how choices are made that result in separations—choices to die, to separate at college, and to give a child up for adoption were absorbing issues. Around this time, she began asking many questions about her birth mother and whether this woman were still living. I think she wanted a back-up. She insisted she did not have a birth father.

Children often work through trauma by focusing on their issues with animals rather than people. It can be less threatening this way. My daughter at this time claimed rights to all the family pets, a Border collie named Blackie and two cats, Coco and Thunder. These animals had learned to dodge her when she was a toddler. They were more tolerant of her than affectionate, but cooperated with being dressed in doll outfits and wheeled around in carriages—when she could catch them. They were older and could die anytime. I think she felt anyone or anything older than she could die at anytime.[20]

The only pet that was totally her own was a cream-colored rabbit named Cloudy. She played with death through Cloudy. She gave him away to a neighbor who kept a dozen or so rabbits, "because Cloudy would be happier with other rabbits." Then she visited Cloudy almost every day, keeping careful track of the multitudinous births, deaths, and give-aways of that rabbit family.

As fall came, I was still sad much of the time and wanted to bring new life into the house. As an attempt to do so, we attended our first party since Pete's death. It took place at a summer house deep in the woods. Walking up the long dirt drive, we could hear the laughter and see the lights piercing the forest. Nice, lively people spilled over the porches and crammed around tables scattered throughout the cottage, drawn inside by delicious smells. I found navigating through that sea of good cheer to be almost unbearable.

I ended up leaving the party at eleven in the evening and impulsively driving 200 miles through the quiet night to a distant town, glad to be alone. The next morning, I purchased identical twin white Manx kitten brothers and drove home. Each had one blue and one copper-colored eye. These two white tornadoes were presented to my daughter as her own. It was a great idea, helping us see that the future contained new life as well as death. Right now we needed our new life to be tender and vulnerable, like ourselves. We were not ready for a raucous party. Maybe that shouldn't have been a surprise, but it was.

During this time, family visiting was frequent. Although my family is scattered across the Northeast, Midwest, and South, someone was at my folks' house at least every other weekend. Brothers and sisters visited each other.

Pete's son came to see me. In the dark, cool basement of my office we sorted through his father's few things. There was clothing mostly and reams of yellowing paper records. We were surprised by the occasional modest memento that Pete had treasured. There was so little. We worked mostly silently, choked by tears. We shipped something of Pete's to each family member.

Since Pete was indigent, his estate was comparatively simple. I was executor; this meant writing letters to get junk mail to stop and creditors to desist. It continued to be hard to get unexpected mail in his name. Pete was able to leave a nice nest egg of life insurance to his son. I know this, at least, must have given my brother satisfaction. The lawyer handled the estate, which although simple took over a year to settle, basically for free. And all the business people, bureaucrats, and clerks involved were sensitive and kind. Telling these strangers a bit of Pete's story and hearing their compassionate responses helped with my healing.

Several casual acquaintances of Pete's in Las Vegas (a bank teller, a grocery store clerk, and his landlord) tracked us down and expressed their admiration for Pete, particularly his friendliness and warmth to the working person. These letters meant a lot.

The Las Vegas police called to ask if one of their officers could purchase the gun Pete used in his dying. We had previously indicated that we wanted the gun destroyed, but Pete's son now gave permission for them to buy it. Their request disturbed me. It is unsettling that something that has caused such sorrow is still on the loose. I held my silence about my concerns.

At the time of his death, Pete wrote notes to his son, parents, girlfriend, and each of his siblings. His letters while he was alive were usually two sentences long; these suicide letters were about a page long. We studied every word. I suppose suicide notes never convey enough information. Pete's note to me stated how he wished to dispose of his goods and directed me how to activate his life insurance. He thanked me and Charleene for our friendship. There was no explanation—none would have been sufficient. There was no "I will always love you"—that would have helped, I think.

The early stages of grief often block out much of the sense of the loved one's existence. Those left behind strive to maintain the sense of connection. They try to burn into their memory all that they know about the departed. It is unbearable to think that the deceased may simply not exist anymore, or even that they are now in an afterlife and becoming interested in other things, moving on from interest in us.

I had a recurring crazy concern. If Pete was on the other side, could he see all my faults which I usually consider hidden? And knowing me as I really am, did he still love me and want to see me again? Or was he disgusted by my imperfection? I knew that he had always had very black-and-white, perfectionist standards. This worry may seem a strange preoccupation, but it was important to me. My logic was that if there is an afterlife, then I would meet him again. I could endure this temporary separation and relish our ecstatic reunion. But if he no longer sought to be my friend and brother, then I had lost him forever. That possibility brought with it a crushing sorrow.

While I knew it is healthy and normal to feel anger at the deceased, particularly in suicide, I wasn't aware of very much anger. I couldn't bear it—I loved him in many ways like a father loves his son. Blended with this was the love I had for him as a brother, as father and mother to me early in my life, and as my teacher and mentor later on. I did have anger at him for not getting his ass back to school earlier in his life when he had the option. So he found school horribly boring; many of us have knuckled under to that!

I experienced another anger immediately after his death. The day after his death, I felt a sharp sense of his cheating me out of being able to take the suicide option myself at some time in the future. I knew the family could never get over two suicides. It was like he had let go of his end of the rope suddenly in tug-of-war, and that was grossly unfair. He broke free and I was stuck here no matter what happened. This anger was drowned within days by my own sadness as we went through the funeral process.

This feeling of being stuck here was an important emotion to notice. It came from my own experience with severe depression, starting when I was ten and continuing through my early thirties. Over that long span there were many times when suicide looked attractive as way to get the hurting to stop. It was most tempting when it seemed a way to end the tiredness that such a long struggle involves.

Therapy, meditation, loving relationships, and hope that my mood would change all helped keep me here. Yet the most important reasons for me to keep living during those decades of despair were threefold: my sense of meaning, my curiosity, and my appreciation for beauty. I have always been blessed with the knowledge that my actions often helped others and found this a very meaningful reason to stay alive. Secondly, I have always had a driving desire to know and understand more. And thirdly, I have the capacity to be deeply transported by the beauty of nature and music. These three attributes never vanished for more than weeks at a time during all those years.

I suspect most people have considered suicide occasionally—some mildly, many seriously. There is such shame felt at having the thought and such panic at hearing it expressed that these deliberations are almost always kept private, deep within our hearts. I have had a great number of clients say, "If I were suicidal I wouldn't tell my therapist or anyone because I would be afraid that they would commit me to a mental hospital." Underlying that thought, I suspect, is a more threatening fear that having these thoughts makes me so different from the rest of the human community (except for its failures) that it means I am not fit to be loved and respected.

As a society, we need to change this silence, one person at

a time. Because the very act of sharing such thoughts allows healing to start. Through talking we can vent the emotional pressure cooker, be reminded of our value, be helped to see options, and, most importantly, be understood and accepted. Until we can freely talk about it, children, teenagers, the elderly, the alone, and all those who are depressed have to carry the burden of suicidal thoughts by themselves. And many will not be strong enough. To help the people who are hurting to talk, we must listen (defined as: to hear oneself or another with thoughtful, nonjudging attention). And we must have the courage to accept that for some, as for Pete, this will not be enough.

While there was little anger consciously directed at Pete, in those first few months there was plenty of anger in me about almost everything else! I was glad to see my anger softening by the end of the summer. My remaining anger seemed to surface spontaneously from deep in my psyche at unexpected times.

Anger turned inward is a cause of depression. So, I guess directing my anger outward was good. But it was very uncomfortable. Growing up in our family, politeness and respect were emphasized. My parents never seemed to argue. As a therapist I was trained to hold back my own feelings while encouraging others to express themselves. Now my own fury demanded to be felt and voiced.

Some feel that much of the pain of grieving is not from the loss of the loved one. Pain comes also from trying to harden one's heart against current feelings and future losses. I tend to agree. After all, the first three months of agony occurred before we could really *miss* Pete; if he were still alive, three months could have gone by between visits without distress.

It is a strange concept. Much of the emotional torment immediately after death is based on anticipation of the future. If the person had gone away for long trip around the world, we would miss him but not be devastated. It is amazing to me, how much our *idea* of what *will* happen often colors how we feel today.

In my desire to find out how Pete was doing, I scheduled another channeling at this time. It was astonishing how well the session spoke to my concerns of whether Pete would still want to associate with me on the other side. It also gives a glimpse of what existence for the departed may be like in the Earth-weeks after death, at least when one leaves the Earth via suicide. Excerpts from the session follow.

November 1991

[This session occurred three months after Pete's death. I indicated desire to connect with Pete if possible. Also, I asked for comments on what was happening within me. I received quite a lot of information about Pete and also got a therapeutic talking to!]

At this time, Pete is very willing to detach from what is here and from what was his darkness. It is very much a not wanting to be attached at this point to the physical plane, so that he doesn't have to be reminded . . . they still show the pull and weeping of the physical.

He is not, Joe, longing to see anyone particularly but you. He has some unresolved issues about his problems. He feels still less of a man. He feels most embittered, as if God had let him down.

Now as we are carrying him beyond this current state of powerlessness, he wishes to carry male to the light. You, Joe, need to see how your current feelings of powerlessness are reactionary to his, for there is still a heart-link between you. And in this linking, my child, there is a draining of self, as you feel somewhat castrated yourself and fear that you and God may have let everyone down.

Now you, Joe, do stand as a giant of light. You have been the emotional carrier for your entire extended family and the weightiness of it has carried you to where it was not personally safe for yourself. You were always willing to go way out on the limb for another.

Joe, the more you bend over to emotionally receive a spanking for not being the performer of all of God's acts, the more humbling the darkness would become for you. We would suggest that you would instead experience the light through the physical now. And it would be through man-hood, and the pleasures that the physical can bring that God would like to heal you at this time. Release the fear that you have missed the mark and there will be instantly a new day dawning. It will come to you, my beloved, as a knowing and there will be gentle peace within your heart once more.

They are showing me that love of the heart is the answer. In peaceful situations, you can feel the light working on your heart. We would suggest, my child, that the more peaceful you become, the more the spirit will be felt by you. And it is through the feeling center that your bleeding heart will be healed.

My child, Pete is finished with the idea that he deserved sadness. He won't be looking for the darkness anymore, for he has come to believe his darkness was cleansed by his suffering in the physical. So he has seen within himself a certain amount of debt paid back. This does clear the way for easier learning. And for a reincarnation next time with gifts to give others. This is what the plan looks like that is unfolding now. He will come back to give back the gener-osities he had received.

My beloved Joe, do you see how your healing has aided him? For as he does remember you nourishing him, this allows him to remember what kindness light gives. So, memories of your kindness do remain behind with him as the darkness shifts to light.

It is your strong desire to do God's work but we would remind you that sometimes God's work goes way beyond your understanding. And your brother chose to join Him before he felt it was too late. Pete did feel that if he were to remain karmically bound too long, his bitterness would have grown so strong that he may have lost a sense of the light altogether. And as God would call him home in love, he felt that he must scurry to get there. We would suggest that you do adjust your perception to knowing that, as love is everlasting and as God is all-knowing, that there are always periods of transition, not death.

Now, there is another person here who is saying that the shock to your system, Joe, was great. You felt that Pete's struggle was going to be guided or governed by the light.

They are saying that you could not come totally to terms with the shock of it—of what he has chosen. And this has caused a numbing of parts around your heart and brain.

Letting go of the need to be the one who makes everybody okay will let you spend more time realizing the heaviness of the responsibility that you carried in your heart for Pete. You need to understand how powerful the guilt and concern was, even when he was alive. And once you see how loaded down you were emotionally by that, they said almost to the point, Joe, of being bankrupt emotionally, you will understand more clearly your feelings of powerlessness that have got a grip on you now.

Do you know what they are showing a picture of now? They show gunshot holes in you, in your heart and in your power center—and if you could see the picture of it, you would say, "Oh God," and you would stop it. Because that puts together your body again and allows you to rebuild all of your energy which you use in tremendously light ways!

They would rather see you quite angry. And to release a lot of your grieving through that. And this is where they are showing the chopping wood and a lot of physical activity to burn some of this off. It is okay to say "I am angry" and not try to have a spiritual view for now.

What Pete still treasures is what you taught him about giving and receiving. Something very good happened there. And it is that which he plans to re-live in his next incarnation. So it is the gift that you gave him, Joe.

Now, when he was here, he saw you as both the savior and a demon. As a savior you were absolutely fabulous, you were like an angel there. And then in a sense you would become a demon to him because he would say, "No, I can't really receive all of this goodness." What he sees on the other side is that your strong savior qualities were the most stabilizing influence he had toward the end. His decision to die would have been made earlier, Joe, except for you. Your intervention helped him grow a little bit more before his death.

So, he got a perspective that he would not have had the chance to get. He would have died totally embittered with all shadows, and with no sense of what light is about. And so from his perspective, he sees you as a stabilizing force for him. He sees you now meandering a bit in trying to find a safe connection for yourself in the physical.

I think I might be getting Pete directly here. Pete says that pride in yourself, Joe, is very important. He says that it is important for you to move on. This is not a family trait to have a lot of pride. If he could have allowed himself a sense of pride about his humanity, about his sensitivity, about his softness, about the good of him—that would have saved him. But he never really allowed himself to do anything that he could be proud of. You need to claim back pride, not just in yourself as a man, but also in what you have been able to create in your life.

You prolonged his life. You kept him on a life-support system. You weren't fully aware of it at the time, but he was nearly brain-dead and you kept pumping in and keeping everything going so he could get more information. He knew ultimately that he could not physically and emotionally be responsible for his actions. He knew that eventually he was going to lose it. It was just a matter of timing. But you gave him a lot of powerful information and you came in and filled in like a father, where he couldn't have gotten that from anyone.

He says that performance is part of your struggle, Joe. That first piece is about performance and the feeling of failure because that feeds into your worrying about whether he will be happy to see you again—that you have failed him.

You would be the first man he gave his Christmas package to, for in this package would be pride in yourself. Because the man of light that is you has surfaced. And now he would be knowing the Christ because he met him through you, Joe.

This man Pete wants no remorse over his passing, for he does not want more guilt showered on his life. He feels more remorse than anything and does not dare to judge you or another, for he feels at times himself so incomplete that he cannot make appropriate judgments. This is the dark shadow we are now removing from him. The only bag of gold he carries now is the love you gave him. He shudders to think that one would judge another, as he knows now that God has not judged him.

And as he removes himself from the blanket of darkness, he would rush back to you, the only man that stood as light in the desert, and hand you his package of serenity. He is letting his guilt go. What he is amazed by is that nobody is judging him. He takes the word "judgment" and has a huge line through it—"no judging." No judgment because his message to you is, his life was all about judging himself unfairly.

He knows that the way to light now is through the heart and he knows that he got caught in defeat and could not allow himself the way home to his heart. He is saying that wherever the wind blows and wherever your seed lands in your quest for the heart—that is fertile ground.

It is the feelings that are going to bring you to peace. Where you are is you have got to allow the anger. You have got to face the fact about how much it has taken from you. There is going to be a lot of anger, there is going to be a lot of weeping, and there is going to be "What is the use anyway." You gave love—but it is God and that individual that makes something happen. And so it is going to help you with a whole lot of detachment.

The message from Pete is real clear about taking pride in what you do. Claim it. And that there was no way that he could understand that. But that everything that you did made a difference right before his death to bring him to the point where he could start to learn love a bit. And there is a real strong need for him to be released, because he doesn't want any more guilt or pain in the physical, even around his name.

So that is what the channeled source said of Pete's status and my condition three months after his death. This message helped me gradually see the possibility that his suicide was not a great defeat for Pete, but rather a way for him to grow past issues that haunted him for lifetimes. The possibility that I had helped him see the reality of love soothed much of my own agony about having failed him. The channeled comments about my own condition and what needed to be done rang true in my heart.

SPRING IS RETURNING
September 20, 1991
My Mother's birthday

Spring is returning in the fall.
Some peace is returning to us all.

This spring fights with hard winter,
Erratic in its victories.

The sky blues after midsummer dullness.
And leaves turn slowly to splendor.

We've had our first birthday
After brother's death day.
Mother smiles in eighty candle light.

Beauty calls softly, again we can hear it.
We are sensitive to each other
And softer with self.

Rage is waning this Sunday night.

8 ∞ SEARCHING

Six months after my brother's death, we had made it through the major holidays and his birthday. It was not an easy period. Thanksgiving surprised me with its difficulty. That day was usually not a big deal most years. I don't know if it was hard because it was the first big family holiday after his death, or because one was supposed to be thankful on that day.

At least by then my family knew when sadness was descending. And we had developed ways to function as a unit to deal with it. By now we had given up fighting so hard to resist grief's presence. That freed up a lot of energy for more constructive purposes. We could go with the flow when anguish appeared. By now we were confident that each particular period of sadness would end. Yet sorrow continued to interrupt our lives. It appeared as an unwelcome guest, particularly when we let our guard down, as one must often do when trying to relax or to celebrate something. I wanted grief to just completely and finally go away. And I hoped that whenever I would think of my brother in the future, it could be with a smile of delight at knowing him and a sense of peace.

Talking about hope brings up the issue of fear. I think my biggest fear during this time was that someone else really close, such as one of my parents, would die. The advantage of sudden death of a loved one is that you enter into the loss with an average amount of energy and are protected by shock for a while. The mind lets it sink in at a protectively slow pace. Now, the fear was that I would have to face another death with defenses torn and little energy left to deal with it.

I was struggling to understand death and how I felt about it. Much of my thinking was muddled and brooding. I was taking it personally, resenting death, and rebelling against its inevitability. So I decided to sit down and take a full look at my attitudes toward death without censoring myself as to good, bad, silly, or brilliant. Six months after my brother's death, here's what I wrote in a brainstorming fashion. Later that same night I went back and italicized the parts of my answer that seemed most powerful or central to me. The questions asked were suggested by the book *Rituals for Living and Dying* by David Feinstein and Peg Elliot Mayo.[21]

How do I feel deep down about my own death?

I think it stinks! I want to know more about what happens and to have an easy dying at a time of my own choosing. *I think we should all get a choice* and be informed of what comes after death. Why not? It would probably make us live life better. I hate not having any control over something that will affect me so deeply. I cannot even promise my own daughter that I will be here while she grows up.

Why do we die?

Our bodies break down—entropy up close and personal! Sometimes people withdraw their own life force. Nature seems to want change. Change equals life, so older organisms are obsolete, *new models are valued over old.* I would like to believe that *we live to learn and die to remember,* as a fifteen-year-old boy once told me.

What is death?

End, beginning? *unfulfilled* goals and unexperienced experiences, black, silence, fearsome, *lack of control,* sorrow for others, emptiness, missing the Spring, *rest,* welcome relief from pain, unfair trickery, plentiful, disease, fear, weakness, surrender, *unwanted,* unnecessary? gateway, eclipse, *mysterious,* sweet, peaceful.

I fear that it will be nonexistence more than I fear a hell, though I am uneasy about hell too. I don't like the loss of ego. *How much sense of self do you keep anyway—better be a lot!*

Different rules, possible traps, death may call on skills of an unknown nature. I feel it is an advantage to be intelligent which I am, and trusting which I may or may not be. I'd like to believe that you are conscious throughout the whole process, peaceful and loving—and have a chance to rest on the other side as long as you want. I want no struggle, great wisdom, *all my questions answered*, then be free to decide whether to live again and have the choice between Earth existence and continuing some other way (angel?).

The veil—I'd like to be able to see my loved ones remaining here and let them know that I am OK and that I love them. *I fear aloneness during dying and after death.* Hope the next existence isn't so hard but just as real and filled with as much beauty. The robber, the thief, the enemy, failure. Could be an ecstatic experience. I have seven more tough deaths to go through, if the people I love die in order of age. I think it gets easier after you have experienced your first significant grief. When you are older, do you yield to death with greater acceptance?

What happens when we die?

I am not sure. I think it is most likely and most desirable that we are greeted by loved ones, feel peaceful, have a rest period, and decide on what we want to do next. But do we forget how difficult it is down here on Earth in our euphoria and sign up for another challenging life too eagerly? Perhaps we get in touch with other-life memories. Can there be love without judgment? Most come back to Earth for another round based on what experience they want, or to be with a person that they are still attached to. Some come back mainly to be of service to others here. But I fear that *there is a danger of forgetting what you have learned previously* and having a terrible life after a good one. Can you slip back in your progress? Progress to what? I don't know. But I feel that *one's life continues forever* in some form, with or without a physical body.

If some of what I want to be true is true, then death can be a beautiful thing. We would get to start over, deep inside knowing what we have learned from the past, yet able to start again with a freshness and an innocence. From what I've gathered, the majority of the world's people, now and in the past, believe in life after death. And most, including a majority of Christians, unofficially consider some form of reincarnation to be the most likely possibility. Brain Weiss's book *Many Lives, Many Masters*[22] is a good introduction to the idea of reincarnation. But majority rule is an uncomfortable way to decide such a question. There is so little hard data, and it is of such importance to us all. Hopefully we have a collective wisdom.

In two decades of working as a psychotherapist, I have listened to many reports from clients about their connections and "conversations" with loved ones who have died. And now my family's own experiences at Christmas and many other times since my brother's death suggest to me an afterlife. Most experiences are subtle. Taken singly, they are easily dismissed as coincidences or random anomalies. Taken together, they have great power.

My family members felt strong feelings of Pete's presence at odd times—usually when they were not thinking about him but were involved in something that Pete was highly interested in when he was alive. For example, months after Pete's death, I sat down with my daughter to teach her for the first time the game of poker. We sat cross-legged in the living room on a beautiful blue silk carpet. Sunlight warmed and brightened our square of rug. We both were relaxed and playful. Beaming delight, she won every single hand from start to finish for more than a one-hour period. This is highly unusual in poker. About halfway through, I felt a strong sense of Pete, an excellent poker player, helping her. It felt like he was making a big affectionate joke. I could almost hear him laughing.

When I would think of Pete as sad and defeated, I didn't feel any connection with him. But I did feel a strong presence occasionally when I would imagine him as transformed into a light and free being, but still Pete. Often my sense of him in these "encounters" was that he was happy and playful. But even using all my meditation and Lifeline techniques, these encounters were disappointingly fragmentary. There were no long conversations, no robust exchange of ideas. I think that I was still too emotionally hot to get into the receptive state needed. Frustrating!

After the holidays, it was time to stop trying to live in two worlds at once. Wondering about Pete and where he might be produced a disconnection from the physical. My body was restless from so much thinking. I shifted to a simpler mode. As part of my grieving process I started to chop wood, take long walks—anything physical. My body sang back its gratitude to me through the joy of muscle and sinew, and fresh air pulled deep into the lungs.

My emphasis shifted from caring for others to taking care of myself. I began to understand more deeply what had happened to me and how I was being changed by this experience.

By the end of January, two things were clear. The first was that suicide was going to be totally and forever unacceptable as an option for me because I now understood the pain it caused others. Also, I had decided that, whatever happened, I would stay around for the ride. I would learn to flow better with pain if I must, but I would be here for the duration. Given the permanency of death at least in this physical body, we die soon enough.

This new clarity represented the end of a way out that I had always kept in the back of my mind somewhere. It was replaced with a sense of obligation to myself to live fully. It was no longer acceptable to put off current experience, in hopes of future reward, or to live through a persona, the mask of what I believe others expect of me.

The second thing that became clear in the gut was that no matter how much I examined them, death and life were going to essentially remain puzzles. I gradually moved from resenting the lack of verifiable information, to an acceptance of mystery, and on to a celebration of mystery. We often pretend to understand, but can only understand from certain specific levels such as the scientific, and this does not fully capture the entire reality of even the simplest organism on this planet. On my good days, I was grateful and thrilled that we are blessed with the ineffable, the unspeakable, the unknown.

Desire to experience life remained, but the compulsion to understand vanished. I am going to rely on curiosity to get me through whatever comes along. Regardless of what pain or fear I might be in, I can be curious about the experience and relish staying in the experience because of that fact. For example, in Aruba my wife wanted to go on a tiny submarine to see the coral reefs. I went and saw the amazing undersea world there, using curiosity to balance my considerable motion sickness and claustrophobia that the small space, the state of being underwater, and the lack of sweet air produced. I am glad I went.

I continue to be eager for the next "went" that will come along. Since my brother's death, I more directly face my fears and explore life versus analyze it. This is a great victory for me.

So the three main reasons that keep me alive during my own decades of depression were each changed substantially by Pete's death. My sense of meaning was no longer tied so tightly to helping others. While helping is still a pleasure, now fulfilling my *self* is a greater priority. I have found that these two things conflict much less often than I would have anticipated. Also, my sense of curiosity ceased to be a drive to understand everything. Now it is more focused upon discovering and celebrating mystery. Finally, my appreciation of beauty deepened in intensity and widened to include the more humble things, such as the architecture of a simple kitchen chair.

By six months after Pete's death I was just beginning to realize the value of these gifts that grief had brought to me.

THE HOLIDAYS
January 15, 1992

Grief deepens as the festival approaches.
Sorrow gashes us when we are least looking,

A small restaurant dinner is planned.
As we dress, tempers flare.
No one wants to go.

Each is afraid to cancel Thanksgiving.
Except child Sarah—she says boldly,
"If no one wants to, why are we going?"

Father has no clear answer.
I just know that we must.
We go and sit down, somber.

I finally make a weak attempt.
It is all I can think of.

"Let's speak out loud
Of something we're thankful.

We start slowly, yet it does lift our mood.
Our world flows with blessings,
Our lives do go on.

We feed on bittersweet memories.
Weaving celebration with each other's help.

I zig-zag to sleep that night wondering,
If this is Thanksgiving, what would Yuletide be like.

Pete's absence shows up often in the next few weeks.
The Season looms, rather than beckons.

We each pull to build Christmas for the other,
Straining at the yoke—up the gray, cold, and muddy hill.

Our family gathers in separate places—
And Magic happens that Christmas eve night.
Each gathering is bathed in great light.

I wonder about love, gentle birth, and renewal,
Connection yet freedom for fresh starts.
New and ancient—through infinity.

New Year's eve finds lovers exhausted and sad.
Mad too, at each other for behaving so bad.

We talk, bleeding and weak.
We go to bed at ten, too tired to speak.

Yet we do so as friends, beat by common foe.
We just yield to grief, not knowing where next to go.

Then surprise!
New Years day feels good and bright.

So we enter a new year
Bowed yet intrigued

Healing-other work is put on hold,
I shift to reading, wood splitting, and sleep.
Solitary healing of wounds so deep.

I sense progress in some way
Yet any impression is good for a day.

I know each of us will try our best
To be constructive until we rest.

And no one would dare to quit early
Now that we know what it is like to be left.

9 ∞ LOST

While Pete was living at our office, in a funny way he and I danced a struggle around dress. He was impeccable in this area, and I was oblivious. Several times while I was at work, supposedly looking professional, he caught me with two different-colored socks on, dark black and dark blue. Twice he was distressed to find me, ready to see clients, in two different-colored shoes, dark brown and cordovan. All I could do was smile sheepishly and plead a dark morning bedroom and too little sleep. Then we would both laugh. At other times I would kid him by trying to mess up his hair.

Now, in the February after his death, I was all excited about going on television as a guest speaker for the first time. Very nervous about how I would look, I stood in my closet, reaching to pick out my tie. Some of the ties I had to choose from were Pete's. A great wave of grief hit me. Pete would have loved helping me select what to wear for this event, and I would have felt confident wearing his choices. More importantly, we would have shared all the aliveness of my TV debut.

In the grey of a seemingly always cold and rainy winter, I really *missed* my brother in the sense that it had been a long time since I have seen him.

Our society doesn't really focus much on brother-to-brother relations. Or, for that matter, sister-sister and sister-brother pairs. Movies, plays, and books seem to focus more on parent-child and spousal relationships. Odd, when you think about it since sibling relationships are important.

The dynamics of parent-child relations are beautiful and essential to the continuation and progress of human-kind, but the richness of intimacy that is experienced in these relations is often limited. The influence and support of your parents—highly important when you are young—often fade, and you may find yourself spending at least half of your life without them. Likewise, kids are parents' most intense focus for two decades, but then they hopefully leave home and create their own lives. Limiting the parent-child relationship also is the divisiveness of generational differences in values and experiences and an inequality of authority and power. There tends to be a one-sidedness to parent-child relations. Parents give to the needy child; then, after perhaps a period of some form of equality, later the adult-child often gives to a needy parent. Yet, despite these limitations, the parent-child relationship, in our culture, is the most sanctified.

Spousal relations, of course, are also essential to the continuation of humankind, and between spouses more intimacy is possible. Spouses usually select each other, are of the same generation, share the bond of sexual union, create and sustain a home, and parent together. These are very deep bonds indeed, often lasting throughout adulthood. There are also a few obvious challenges to intimacy here, however. Spouses do not bond from birth as parent-child pairs do. Moreover, spouses are often selected to be complementary to us (if we are quiet, we tend to marry someone outgoing), yet the complementary easily becomes the conflictual. Spouses are also often selected unconsciously to complete unfinished issues in the parent-child relationship, creating ongoing struggles between partners. Furthermore, spouses are sometimes selected for evanescent reasons, such as a desire to escape the parental home.

A relationship between brothers—between any siblings—has the potential for far fewer limitations and obstacles. Of course not all, and perhaps not many, brother relationships realize their potential; many relationships start out weakly and need blessed conditions initially to grow strong and resilient—much like the path of acorn to the oak. The fulfilling sibling relationship requires the consistent consent and desire of both parties and the encouragement of the surrounding community.

Given the proper environment, being brothers can be a deeply intimate and enriching experience. The bonding starts at birth for one brother and usually very young for the other. Unless adopted or step-children, they are united by the closest possible genetics, closer even than parent-child. They are further united by generational closeness and common teaching of culture and values by their parents. They share a common joy and sometimes a common enemy on a daily basis, as they react to their parenting situation. Their relationship extends from birth to death—frequently many more years longer than parental or spousal relationships. By adulthood, authority and rivalry issues have usually softened, allowing a true friendship where physical affection is possible without the complications of overt sexuality.

Brothers can easily become best of friends, confidantes, mutual mentors, a place of refuge from the struggles with parents and spouses, helpers with decision-making and supporters of those decisions. They can keep their family and individual histories alive for each other. A brother is someone with whom you can be fully honest about defeats, fears, imperfections. You can ask without shame for a loan—of money, car, time, or energy. Brothers are usually good repositories of secrets, particularly about deep feelings concerning the parent or spouse. Brothers usually have a code of silence allowing trust that, whatever tender issue is expressed, it will be kept private. Trust is further encouraged by the absence of the threat of retaliation that exists in the power dynamics of parent-child and spousal relationships.

While we have Mother's Day, Father's Day, and wedding anniversaries, we do not celebrate a Brother's Day or a Sister's Day. Why do we not more vigorously acknowledge, encourage, and celebrate siblings? On the one hand, perhaps it is best. The fact that I have celebrated my siblings with something more akin to internal prayer than to public celebration has kept rituals from trivializing feelings from the heart. On the other hand, rituals allow us to acknowledge perceptions that are more than facts and memories, perceptions that are facets of myth and imagination. And a myth of brotherhood may be important personally and culturally.

Myths color our perception of reality and allow us space for creativity and problem solving. Our myths become models for our behavior. Because we emphasize the parent myth so intensively, we confine ourselves to approaching all relationships from this perspective. God becomes god the father; bosses become fathers and employees become children. We look for mothering and fathering from our spouses. We look to government to be the good mother (nurturing and undemanding of us) and the good father (protective and enabling). We fear our government is becoming the bad mother (intrusive, controlling, and draining) and the bad father (self-absorbed, punitive, arbitrary, and violent). We feel as helpless and pessimistic as little children to change our government-parent. We feel no sense of control over our government and therefore have none. In our relationship with the Earth, too, we can see the effects of the parent model. When we view the Earth as mother, there is a danger of taking too much from her and returning too little, as children do.

If we expanded, celebrated, and applied the myth of brotherhood, many more options would open to us. What changes would happen in business if boss and employee, businessperson and customer related to each other as brothers? What changes in government would occur if bureaucrat and taxpayer were brothers? What if we viewed the Earth as brother as well as mother? What would it be like to relate to God as brother or sister? Bringing brotherhood into these relationships may help us remain sensitive to dimensions of fairness, balance, reciprocity, kindness, cooperation, and mutual power. We may see options where it appeared before there were none.

Since my brother's death, I am sensitized to the dimensions of brotherhood playing out in all aspects of life. It is in our power to enhance our appreciation of brotherhood in our relations with siblings, spouses, and friends. We can then extend this outward to change the impasse we feel with our institutions and to deepen our relationship with our Earth and our God. The brotherhood myth truly may have the potential to guide us from childhood into fully mature human adulthood.

All this musing is terribly abstract—in this February, seven months after his death, I missed Pete deeply. Part of my soul was torn and my heart was broken. I have other brothers and a sister whom I value highly, but Pete was gone and he was irreplaceable. I missed his smell, hands, smile, advice, humor, and interest in my life; I missed his help, and I missed helping him. I felt incomplete at my core. I longed for him at a place deep inside where I have never longed for a lover.

The yearning hit at odd times. Shock had given way to fatigue. Nothing had ever before produced such a tiredness of spirit in me—not mononucleosis, not 130-hour weeks in graduate school, not waking up several times a night for months with a sick child. At that moment, deep in winter, it felt as though relief and rest would never come. Warmth and life seemed to have permanently died much of the time. There was a sense of being out of control and unable to change the scenario of grief, loss, and lack.

I felt a sense of community with the many that I have never met who are struggling in the absence of a spouse, child, or best friend—all players in the symphony of grief. And I knew I was in the percussion section, which speaks loudly but not often of the grief of a lost brother. My heart beat with the rhythm of these drums. The closest rhythm to this I had felt before was the drums pounding in muted profundity during President Kennedy's funeral procession. They accurately captured the sadness and the length of the march. They echoed the loss of hope.

At that point I'd have been grateful for any after-life that provides rest and reunion with all those I have come to love. But that was for later. For my daughter's sake and for my own, I needed to struggle back to life on the surface again. I would take as much rest as I could find, when I could find it. But I had to keep marching forward.

Here's what Pam's channelings were saying during this period of my grieving:

You respond sometimes to Pete's old self, and when you do that you reconnect with the darker side of yourself which is always located in the heart near Pete and Pete's death. So in a lot of ways what you are going through is the birthing of a new man, and the death of the old. That is why there is so much sense of the loss—the emotions get mixed up with the loss of your old self but also the significant loss of Pete.

And whenever you have a problem with that, it is like your energy connects with old energy patterns of Pete's. Not Pete as spirit now, but the remnants of Pete's energies, which still hang around a bit, because the whole grieving process is not completed. And they want you (this is a very clear picture) to see that they are separate things—that Pete's soul energy is way beyond the physical. Pete's soul energy is way beyond the ideas of loss.

As a matter of fact, they show him in a marching band. He is having the time of his life, OK? But his ego remnants are still clinging in the physical and they tend to cling where the loss is felt the most and really, outside of his mother, it is you. So you need to disconnect from any idea, from any stress related to Pete's disease. And Pete's disease was refusal to allow himself success.

And so the focus is on yourself right now and on letting go of the whole idea that there should be limitation around success. They are saying that as you do this, you will find yourself going through some grieving about Pete's old ways of being. And they are saying that you need to allow pieces of this grieving, but they are saying it is the remnants, all right?

[At this point I asked if this energy remnant had an intelligence to it, like a ghost, or was it just the memory of Pete?]

Ah, it is like a ghost. That energy is very thick. It is not formed like a ghost, but if I were going to say that it is one or the other, I would say it is a ghost, not a memory. So we are talking about a literal energy that hangs around. So see, the minute you start to slip into the shades of you that are a bit like the old Pete, you hook right into it. And Pete's energy is connected to your home. Yes, your home is where you tried to heal him and so that was really his last home.

They show you pulling forth friends and relations who are willing to support this. And they show you building a huge bonfire on your farm. They show you standing around in a circle, hands held, and they show you singing your last farewells to him. You are to show Pete through song that your hearts wish to be free of him now, as you see him in a glorious estate of love.

In other words, he is in another home and in the state of love. And you and your friends on Earth share with each other. There is food. It is like a feast. And they show you shaking hands, communicating, holding one another and talking about your lives and your future. You leave no room for sadness in this new energy field that you are planting. And this bonfire dissolves the ghost-like mist that hangs there. They are showing this energy of Pete's is so thick around there, that when this is gone a lot of the pressure you are under will ease.

The power of the ego is most strong right before death. It attaches to those who are strongly involved with the dying person. It is these attachments on the passing of another that cause great distress for the survivors and the terrible sense of loss.

Be not sad at your brother's death now, but happy at the letting go of the form of his life. This is a great celebration to be had, for it is the dissolving of the energies of his personality which refused to let him alter his life plan. So the form of his unhappiness must and can be dissipated, as each person is willing to release him.

We pass no judgment on the suicidal notion of your brother Pete. But we must make it very clear that the horror of one's life is bound to energies, and unless they are forgiven and let go of, they travel wherever you are. This is the human term of hell. The passing of your brother from the physical was a blessing for him in that he could not escape from the harsh karma of his lifetime.

That bonfire, I have never been so sure of anything, it is so clear it is like my eyes are blazing with it. And that fire does consume the mist. You are talking about a real thing. You can't see it. If you saw a mist over the mountains you'd say, Oh well, the sun just has to burn it off. This fire is going to do the same thing to dissipate old Pete energies.

Feeling a little silly, my wife and I gathered friends and had the recommended bonfire and fellowship. A friend of mine blew notes of sorrow on a conch that echoed through the mountains. I read some of my poetry and found myself weeping. We danced, sang, and said goodbye once again to Pete. I could feel the strong loving as good friends each in turn held me, as the fire died down and the night got cold. Strangely, our house and our moods seemed much lighter after this ritual and that peculiar heaviness never returned. It was a significant step in our moving on.

TIRED AND TENDER
January 20, 1992

Death leaves the living tired and tender.
Twilight time often catches you.
But bright sunlight too, is suspect.
Sweet-ache longing returns again and again.
Even to the strongest of men.

You swim through your sea, rounding to places
Before you shared with the now dead.

The restaurant at the far edge of town,
The closet where clothes were hung.

Tired and tender—those places
Produce a swell of sweet suffering.

You want to remember all you can.
Try to recapture the essence of man.

Each memory, opens the sad scar
Yet gives you him back—he can't be far.

You go through this, there is no choice.
Hoping uncertainly, fearing defeat.

The after-life becomes paramount.
It is the place of reunion
And a rest from so much tiredness.

10 ∞ FULL STOP

About ten months after my brother died, things had quieted down considerably inside of me. But somehow it felt that I hadn't completely said goodbye to Pete. I had not yet let the experience fully penetrate to the center of my being.

I also hadn't been alone for an extended period of time. I am a private person, in the sense of doing my best "getting in touch" when alone, and then, after this solitary encounter, sharing my perceptions with others. But I had been avoiding solitude, overscheduling activities to keep Pete's death from penetrating too deeply.

There was some part of me that was waiting to see his corpse to believe that it actually had happened. Pete's body had been quickly cremated and shipped back East in a six-by-six-inch plain cardboard box, the kind that could have contained mail order vitamins or new parts for a shaver. This box bore no relationship to the brother I knew. My sister shared my discomfort about this aspect to the degree that she wondered if Pete had faked his death to escape creditors and was now living in some foreign land. She reasoned that perhaps my older brother, in collusion with this plan, had lied about identifying Pete's body. Hope does not die easily.

I realized that it was time for me to face reality more deeply. And I needed something to help me do this. I decided to go to the place where Pete had died. I scheduled a five-day trip to Las Vegas for July, on the one-year anniversary of his death. There, alone and with total anonymity, I could sleep, eat, and cry when I wanted and nobody would really get excited given the daily strange goings-on in that city. I figured any emotional outburst would just look like I had been unlucky at the tables.

It seemed like a good idea at the time.

About two weeks before the trip, anxiety began rising. Two days before I was to head out on my quest, I became clearly afraid. Ahead of me was the unknown. I could not predict what would be experienced, felt, and expressed. Suddenly I did not trust myself to maintain control.

Usually I feel a wonderful excitement at the thought of going someplace alone. For this trip, I had arranged to take good care of myself. First-class airplane reservations were booked for the first time in my life and a nice hotel suite was reserved. Yet now, with the trip imminent, I felt more than alone; I felt lonely.

Anger, disgust, and fear about Las Vegas surfaced. This was a city that I had previously loved for its freedom, friendliness, variety, and excitement. Could I really blame a whole city for somehow not welcoming and saving my brother? Evidently a part of me could. It felt as though Vegas did not care about my brother and would not care about me. It became a place where one could get lost and never return. Las Vegas pulled at me like a black hole.

The morning after arriving in the city, I asked a cabby to drive me to the mortuary that handled my brother's remains. I found myself telling the cabby what was going on; he was quietly sympathetic. The mortuary was round and modern. I entered, palms sweaty, and there was nothing to see but a small reception desk behind a glass window. Its feel was more of a bank than of sacred space. I turned around without saying anything and got back into the cab. My strongest emotion was "He is not here."

I asked the cabby to drive to Pete's old apartment. The last time I had been there, we sat in his apartment and by the pool, enjoying a relaxed intimacy. Now, in midmorning, in the eerie silence of a community where all residents had gone to work, I walked up to his door, then to the pool, and left within five minutes of arriving—not having seen a soul. Again I had a strong sense of "He is not here."

It was bittersweet, remembering the times we had shared

together there. I had planned to walk the neighborhood as we had done together before. Now it felt fruitless.

The cabby took me back to the hotel. The whole trip had taken less than thirty minutes. I had planned on it taking hours, and now I realized that my trip was as much an attempt to find him as to let go of him. I went up to my hotel room and decided to try to get angry or something—to get out what was inside of me. Nothing came.

I felt spent and very tired of focusing on death. I went down to the hotel pool, sat in the shade to avoid the worst of the pounding heat, and wrote the poem that appears at the end of this chapter. It really was time to move on.

The rest of the time in Vegas, at every opportunity I willed myself to let go of this sticky grief. As the elevator rose, I imagined leaving the grief behind on the ground. As I walked down the long hall from the hotel to the casino, I imagined dropping a dull grey cloak of grief behind me, and walked faster—never looking back. I repeated these images often over the days to come. Finally, I began to feel lighter.

I purposefully threw myself into the excitement of the casino, letting the din of coins and flashing lights enfold me. I expansively started conversations with strangers and was extra nice to the casino personnel. They responded warmly. When I got tired I would go up to my bed, enter a relaxed state, and imagine myself floating high above the desert—free of all the responsibility that I had carried toward Pete, free of being responsible for my family's feelings. I took an oath to now live fully, freely, and joyously, even if I forgot Pete totally in the process and lost him forever.

As my stay continued, I did exactly what I felt like doing in each moment, allowing myself to change my mind instantly. Sometimes I slept for thirty minutes, stayed up for twenty minutes, and went back to sleep. Sometimes I stayed up for thirty hours and then slept for ten. I would begin a meal, change my mind, and walk out. For a few days I stopped all the "shoulds"—from showering, shaving, and brushing teeth to any "should" about grieving, caring, or calling home.

This "vacation" was one of the best gifts I had ever given myself. My recommitment to myself and to what life can bestow charged me with great energy. Part of the freedom was fueled by anger. "Well, Pete. You decided to check out, so *Fuck You!*" Part of the freedom was fueled by love. For both of us, our relationship needed to close. It was the only way that the good in the relationship could continue to outweigh the bad. Our relationship was too fabulously beautiful, too sacred, to tarnish it with more regrets, guilt, and sorrow.

Here's what Pam's channelings said about Pete's progress on the other side after I had returned from Vegas:

Let's see . . . now, Pete's energy is watchful of you. He is still . . . it is like he is still in town, he just isn't in your house. And he has a wistful energy about him when he watches you. It is not jealous, it is wistful in the sense that he wishes that he could have gotten himself together but it doesn't come across as a jealousy of what you are doing. It is more his sense of loss.

If you get hooked into that . . . it looks pretty far away from you, but if you find yourself connecting with sort of a wistful "Gee, things just really don't work just the way you want them to," then cleanse yourself. Because he is growing and is freed up considerably to get more light. He is in a weakened state in that he doesn't have as much energy. And this has opened him so that the light can get in. It is like when you are the most vulnerable, when after a good cry someone can really come in and talk to you. That is where he is. So actually in freeing yourself from him and insisting on the distance, he is suddenly being surrounded by more light as he too lets go a little.

[I mentioned writing this book and asked if I should continue because writing it was making me sad.]

When you can laugh out loud at Pete's predicament, you can pull this from the shelf. Until then, the timing would be poor as it would create an open doorway for his re-entry. His energy would seek the book to help redefine himself, and you would be left writing the tears of his life.

So, as you would remove self a bit from this and become very drawn into the physical world . . . They want you to enjoy the physical world, Joe. As you do this, you will find yourself solidified and then able to look back with a luxurious laugh at Peter's predicament and his means of resolving it. They are saying the more grounded you are in the sense of pleasure in the physical, the less Pete's energies can inhibit you. OK? He really doesn't mean to, he is just enormously sad! Your farm home feels freer.

[I asked how at one time they could report he was "playing-in-the-band" happy and at another time report that he was sad.]

I think that they go back and forth in emotions like we do, only it is in another dimension. It is interesting, they are saying that the dead can get greedy for more physical experiences through those who are mourning, as a way to gather more information for themselves to improve their situation—to further their understanding or just to be a part of physical life again. They may not want to let go of physical attachments because, in their sudden deaths, they have lost their means of grounding and of learning. And they are saying that these visitations are not always necessarily good for the mourner. All souls are seeking peace and enlightenment on various dimensions and so, in many ways, life does go on the way it was here.

As you feel the closeness of Pete's old energy, you do have the right to create a free zone for self—and they are showing a huge bubble of light, so that, in Earth terms, the passage of time allows a general healing. Right now, Pete just wishes like crazy that he had been able to pull it off.

This channeling was, of course, encouraging. I put the writing of this book aside, figuring to pick it up in a few months, after I was feeling more solid. It would be two more years before it felt safe to write again. When I finally began again, I was delighted to find that I could write about Pete without sadness.

THE CYCLE IS DONE
July 4, 1992

This is the last poem.
The Cycle is done.

A year has passed.
It's time to move on.

No more waiting at the end of the runway.
The jet left long ago, no trail remains

The sun has set, all is silent.
In fact, new dawn tinges the cold sky.

You are not here, no matter where I look.
Fading memories are not intimacy.

There really is no response.
That's what death means.

By steel will, I drop the grey cloak—
Grief that has covered my heart so long.

It is past time now to radiate with the sun.
The lightness feels so good—alive again.

Angels say I was your father in past times.
This time we fathered each other decently.

I now cut the cord on all this responsibility.
I let go all judgment of our acts.

I embrace incompleteness and mystery.
If loss is forever, so be it.

I hope to connect past the personality
I came to know as my brother.

Linking through the infinite us.
But that must take its own time.

I now drop the old, the dead—and move on.
Into this year's flowers and song.

The moment of silence has passed.
You were honored well by it, but life calls me now.

Engage! Engage! I'm still in the game, you see.
Wife, daughter, and plans call firmly to me.

Life calls that strongly now.
I must risk forgetting you, so that I can live.

Rely on yourself or what else you can find.
I'll be doing the same.

This is hard love.
Terrible in its mystery.

You gave me so much—good bye.
You were so good—I love you.

Wish you the best . . .
We're free . . .

11 ∞ MAPPING THE TERRITORY

By the time I was completing this book, three years after Pete's passing, I was feeling almost fully healed and excited to be growing in many new dimensions. What about Pete? What might his existence be like at this point in time? Of course we cannot know for certain, but this chapter will conclude with the final channeling about him received three years after his death. Some of it suggests what the afterlife might contain for us.

From my loss of Pete, experience with clients, work in meditation, meeting with participants at The Monroe Institute and hearing their experiences, and from reading what seems like countless books over the years, here is my clearest sense of what may actually happen after we die. What I will say occurs in the context of knowing that humans have traditionally believed that there is an afterlife. Egyptian, Tibetan, Hindu, Buddhist, Moslem, Mesoamerican traditions and religions, as well as Judaism and Christianity, all accept life after death.

First, the Near-Death Experience literature appears to be accurate as to what happens during dying. My only personal taste of this was the out-of-body that I experienced during my motorcycle accident. I felt many of the things described in near-death experiences. This experience went a long way in convincing me that the experiences reported are real. Raymond Moody's books[23] and others[24] describe this phenomenon in detail.

These reports of near-death experiences cannot be dismissed as hallucinations caused by neurochemical changes at the time of death. The reports are very different in content and coherence from hallucinations caused by a disturbed brain. The reports often contain information that the unconscious, dying person could not possibly know through ordinary perceptual means, such as which tools the doctors used and what people were doing in adjacent rooms. Commonalities across reported experiences from diverse cultures suggest that we may encounter the following events in any order:

1. We may hear or feel a buzzing sensation.
2. We may find that we exist as energy or in an energy body while still being able to hear and see into the physical world.
3. We may experience an awesome sense or vision of light.
4. We may have feelings of great love, deep peace, and of coming home.
5. We may encounter spiritual beings and perhaps loved ones who have previously died.
6. We may experience a review of our significant life events.

Reports of these near-death experiences are not all positive, but negative experiences seem extremely rare. As we move further in time from the act of dying, there is naturally nothing written from the first-person perspective. Organized religions all have their traditions. Many traditions speak of an initial period spent in cleansing or purification, followed by a period of rest. Many feel that prayers for the dead are helpful and contact between the living and the dead is possible. The Tibetans believed that it was critical to pray for the person for the first month to guide the person to God. A modern book of interest on this subject is the *American Book of the Dead* by E.J. Gold.[25] Most traditions involve the idea that the soul's final destiny is eventual full union with God.

The Monroe Institute offers a series of tapes developed by the expert in death and dying, Elisabeth Kubler-Ross, M.D., by the expert in consciousness Charles Tart, Ph.D., and by the out-of-body expert Robert Monroe. This tape series, called *Going Home,* is designed to help a terminally ill person feel more comfortable and, when the time comes for death, make his transition a loving, peaceful, fearless, and conscious process regardless of his religious orientation. It also provides tapes to assist the loved ones left behind to understand the process more fully and to let go with less pain.

Many traditions allow for reincarnation. In his book *Journey of Souls*, Michael Newton, Ph.D., uses the hypnotic sessions of many subjects to map out a detailed description of the between-lives state.[26] I am personally aware of a few of my past lives. Through my direct experience with the concept, reincarnation has gained credibility for me.

My belief in reincarnation was confirmed because in these memories I knew I was "me" but the quality of my thoughts and emotions had a completely different imprint than what I know as twentieth-century Joe Gallenberger. I felt that I could not be making it up as I went along. One of my memories was unearthed during a session in which my wife gave me a simple instruction, to remember a past life. I relaxed and went through a tunnel. On the other side I looked down at my feet, and then gradually looked up and saw where I was.

I found myself in ancient Egypt, a slave pulling a rope with many other men. The heat and dryness were palpable. I felt a pride in being part of a big project. Charleene asked me what were the names of the men next to me. I didn't know, and it seemed completely unimportant. She asked me how I got there, and I was immediately filled with a deep sadness as the memory of being torn from my tribe overtook me. While this was going on I was struck with how simple and uncomplicated my consciousness was, compared to now. The primitiveness was startling and more than a little bit refreshing.

I told Charleene that this was too intense, I wanted to come back. She suggested instead that I go to when I was younger and immediately I was about five years old with my tribe. The consciousness shift was again amazing. The tribe was linked telepathically as one unit in thought, and its mood alternated dramatically, depending on how close to an oasis it was. I was aware of a very strong imprinting, somewhat similar to modern children knowing to look both ways before crossing a street. The imprint here was "Always know where your water is." I began to feel indescribably tired, and Charleene brought me back to present time.

Another of my past life memories illustrates how we may be influenced by strong thought-forms or addictions and how they may lead to less comfortable incarnations. This one occurred spontaneously during meditation. I suddenly found myself experiencing a rest period between lives. It was dark, and I was deeply sleeping yet aware of being surrounding by many others doing the same thing. A great peace came from the full knowledge that we are not alone. I decided to go back and see what the previous life had been like.

I was surprised to find myself a few-days-old infant, thrown away on a desert trail as my family kept walking. I was disturbed to experience my own death by exposure. I tried to figure what was going on. The mother loved the child but the father said "too many" and dropped me there. Why would I let myself get in that mess? I discovered that, in the life before that one, I had been addicted to a woman. When I died I immediately willed to be with her, not looking at anything else, and dove back into a physical life to follow her. She was an older sister in the family which threw me away, and I got to experience losing her all over again, hopefully by this lesson learning some of the difference between addiction and love.

The Monroe Institute has recently established a new program, called Exploration 27. I had the good fortune to be a co-trainer for the program's maiden voyage. Exploration 27 takes up where Lifeline leaves off. It facilitates participants going into deep meditation and exploring what goes on in the afterlife space called the Park.

From data gathered by these meditators, it seems that when we die there is indeed a period of reunion with loved ones, then a period of rest and rejuvenation. It seems that there are other functions within this consciousness space such as education via simulated experiences, direct knowledge, and observation. Also, there appears to be planning function where one is helped to design further experiences for one's development, including perhaps another Earth lifetime.

Reports from Lifeline, psychics, channelers, and clients all suggest that some people after passing remain attached to or concerned with the physical for at least a while. A good example is from one of my clients after the sudden death of a mother of young children. The client reported seeing the mother nightly in the house where her children were sleeping, until it was decided who would continue the care for her children.

It appears that during the period of rest and rejuvenation contact with loved ones on Earth is least likely or most difficult. When contact is initiated by those they knew on Earth, some of the deceased seem to discourage contact, at least for a while. Many meditators report a first contact with a deceased love one as a joyous reunion; but then, if they pursue frequent contacts, the deceased appears less pleased, as if to say, "Nice to see you but your energy is better spent living than visiting with me."

There are many exceptions to this generality, particularly the frequent reports of a vivid sense of the deceased's consoling presence that seems to occur spontaneously in dreams. During the waking life of the loved one on Earth, contacts come most commonly at stressful times but also occur at happy times. Contacts of this type may continue for decades. But they tend to be very infrequent for most people.

Information from the sources also suggests that the afterlife is filled with the essential quality of all life—change and growth. It appears that in the afterlife experience one still has the opportunity for varieties of emotion. And changes in plans and thoughts may occur, at least in the short term (however that may be defined in a place where time does not appear to exist as we know it).

These sources suggest that we humans are much more than our physical bodies and our conscious minds—that after death, once we break free of any restrictive thought-forms, we become significantly more aware of the fullness of our being which some call our Greater Self or Higher Self. It seems that, because we are aware of the larger picture of our own nature and also the love and connection between all consciousness, even while there is change we have a greater awareness of being essentially safe and loved, and we cease to worry about being judged. This liberating freedom from judgment is explored in detail in an interesting book, *Conversations with God*.[27] Robert Monroe's book, *Ultimate Journey*, published the year before he died, provides his perceptions of what we may find after we finish Earth existence.[28] Most of these sources agree with religious thought that says that the eventual path is to become one with God or realize that the kingdom of heaven is within, that we are already an intimate part of God-source.

My own experiences suggest to me now that dying can be a struggle, but that it doesn't need to be if we are prepared and supported. Then death can be peaceful and natural. I feel that during death we do see the light, meet with someone with whom we feel loved, rest deeply, receive guidance, then usually reincarnate to continue our growth. In exceptional situations, we may go straight to union with God if we are ready, or fairly quickly back to Earth if we are addicted to a particular person or experience. We can be kept stuck by strong thought forms, such as the idea of Judgment Day or karma (as you sow, ye shall reap). But eventually we all merge with God.

I have grown and learned incredible lessons on this journey of grief and discovery following Pete's death. Even with all my religious, clinical, and scientific preparation, my brother's death by suicide still hit me like a ton of bricks. I had to go through the human stages of sorrow, anger, and eventually acceptance. I am now convinced that an afterlife exists and that contact with loved ones who have died is possible. And if accomplished, such contact is a poor substitute for having them alive but will bring the peace of knowing that they are okay.

I know now that the stages of human grief can be used, with grace and support, to bring about tremendous positive changes in one's life. And finally, I know that mystery abounds—we might as well celebrate the fact, rather than living under the delusion that someday some authority will explain everything for us.

The following channeling session occurred three years after Pete's death and is the latest channeled information that I have about him. It occurred during my final re-write of this book.

October 1994

The soul of Pete is more buoyant. It has been freed up. It has a much more angelic quality, which is actually the quality that you related to when you remember him in terms of love and sweetness.

Now he is feeling more free to communicate with you. He has a new kind of consciousness. He is laughing. Now that you are more free of guilt and sadness, he can communicate directly with you. As a matter of fact, he will be a facilitator of a lot of the ideas for moving things around within your book. He is certainly out of sleeping.

And that is the part that I am seeing of Pete that is surviving. He is just getting out of his shell. He is staying very close to the third dimension. I think he will reincarnate. But this is the first taste of freedom that I have ever seen with him. He is totally enjoying. He looks almost cherubic.

He is around you . . . there is a great releasing and what he is showing me is freedom for you. It is like taking your hands off of a plow. He is showing me pictures. The plow is a symbol of work. He is taking your hands off the plow. Higher consciousness does not get involved in work as he did. And it removes itself from the plow. Fundamentally what he is saying is that things don't need to be so hard. Things just aren't that hard. It was just his Earth consciousness that made him believe that it was.

When you have a consciousness of work, then you will, no matter how good a soul you are, have the experience of toil and the disappointment and all the limits that come with work. His kind of suffering does not have anything to do with the goodness of the soul. It has to do with the consciousness around work and the valuing of yourself. He shows you breaking the mold. He has broken the mold in his own way by leaving that behind, by shedding that skin.

Now, don't relate success to goodness of soul. This needs to be a theme in your book. Now, he is showing me a picture, he is going into the well with tears filling up. I think it is related to grief. Yes, there is some grief left back there, more in terms of regret. He is showing grief and it weighs him down. Now he turns into a firefly and the grief puts water in the light, and the little fireflies can't light.

He is going to hang around you, Joe. And he can do that as long as you feel safe with it. There is no heaviness around him at all. The firefly thing seems to be significant. I do not know why. It is sort of an odd image to show me.

He is also saying that he had a real chemical imbalance. So that many of his mood shifts and just his whole psyche were unavoidable. A lot of his pain was just not being able to control that. And it was chemical.

Now, in talking about while he was here, he is saying that he could not forgive himself to experience his passion. Now, he gets back out of that energy to continue to talk to you. He does not like to get into that energy even to mention it. When he gets even close to the energy of that life, it is like getting short of breath. That is how important it is to really release any connection to guilt and judgment.

It is interesting, he feels very free now. I don't suppose that he will create anything like that again. He seems very clear about not drawing up another bad plan for a hard life. He sees it was really a bad plan and from his point of view he also knows that he does not have to draw up the same plan. He is starting to understand choice. He flies like an angel. He is funny. He is enjoying the lightness, the freedom of nonphysical.

12 ∞ I CAN NOW GO LIGHTLY

I have had one more significant release on my journey. Near the second Christmas to follow Pete's death, while I was teaching at The Monroe Institute, a woman offered to perform an ancient American Indian ceremony, called smudging, to help me release my grief. I said, "Sure." A few other women were standing around, heard our plans, and asked to watch. To this I also said, "Sure." We went outside at dusk. The splendid mountain view was fading. The wind sharpened at the top of the hill as we began.

The ceremony is a blur. But at some point these six women formed a circle around me. I have never felt a more powerful, more positive, and safer energy than I did within this circle. Within this energy, without intending to, I began to weep deeply. I had a clear vision of the dance of responsibility and failure that my brother and I had been doing through what felt like aeons of time and hundreds of lives. I screamed and I let this all go. It was finished.

The women then moved in close, supporting my body with their warmth as I collapsed on that cold winter night. They held me upright, swaying and singing gently. I will always remember their loving support. I thank them again here for expanding my knowledge of positive female power and helping me release what may have been a pattern held for a millennium.

Time passed, into another winter. I realized that the past six months had been much better for me. A number of projects had been completed and some new exciting ones were begun. My family was well. The holidays were better this year. But

I had become subtly impenetrable in some hard-to-explain way. I was friendly enough and still cared about people, but part of me had hardened so that no one would hurt me so deeply again. And there was some sense of feeling that in situations of deep pain, it was "every man for himself" because no one else could really help.

I liked this new freedom from responsibility for everyone else's feelings. My wife was the only one who commented on my hardness. She didn't like it. I interpreted her comments as meaning that I was more difficult to manipulate and less easy to predict. I was very engaged in my work and that felt good.

I came to know of my closed-offness in a strange way. It happened in March. I was passionately wrapped up in negotiating for a project that promised to make me happy for decades to come. If it came about, I would be living with a community of friends whom I loved and would be doing work that was perfect for me. Everything seemed to be going well and I was celebrating a done deal. Suddenly I was cut off at the knees; the project fell through. I was devastated. Within minutes, I understood that after my brother's death, I had arranged myself inside to never be ravaged again. But I had thought that death was the only way I could be devastated at such a deep level. I was wrong—here was another way.

Seconds after I realized this, I let myself open wide to this new hurt. For hours I let it flow through me, keeping my defenses down. It felt good, even with all the pain, to not resist, to not struggle to control and contain. I realized that I could stop the loss and save the project by "kissing ass" and compromising a few important values. I didn't. I understood then that I was fully committed to living my own life, not someone else's idea of it. After this all had calmed down, I took a look at what I had discovered about myself and my stance toward letting people hurt me.

I had thought that the key was to learn nonattachment, and I had thought I had mastered this. What I had really done was close off to people and become attached to not feeling any more deep pain. This fear of the agony of loss, if left unchecked, could destroy intimacy and genuineness for the rest of my life.

Yet it was not acceptable to go back to the old position of vulnerability with which I had lived life before my brother's suicide. Very likely, it was not possible. If you have ever lived through an earthquake, the solidity of the ground cannot be taken for granted again, not all the way, deep down. Inside yourself you know that the solid can liquify and change.

I searched fatalistically for a good while for an answer to the question of how to be open and fully engaged with people, and yet not be vulnerable to full devastation once again. It seemed that there was no way out of this dilemma. Then, in a moment of grace, I was surprised to find an answer that had hope of working for me. I trust that the answer will also be useful to others.

It had to do with the idea of completeness and perfection that I feel must be the true reality of things here on Earth. For nearly forty years, I had been perplexed and deeply disturbed by the presence of so much pain in our world. How could a loving God allow it?

Logic dictated that there *was* a God. I could not see a way for inanimate matter to create mind and spirit. The big bang, evolutionary theory and natural selection all could be true, and yet for me could not account for the original something from nothing. Nor could blind random physical events account for the formation of the beauty and complexity of life on this planet.

So for me, there was a God, and often I was awed by the love and intelligence of the Creator. But I feared that he was either dead or cruel to allow so much suffering to proceed unabated in the world. Sometimes, when I was confronted with how much pain exists, religion and faith seemed like just so much whistling in the dark.

I was walking along a country road at The Monroe Institute that spring enjoying birdsong and roadside flowers that glowed a most vibrant blue in the fresh sunshine. Feeling relaxed and happy, suddenly I glimpsed a newborn doe bounding through the field on my left. The doe had been roused by a tractor slowly moving through the field, filling the air with new-mown smells. Thrilled, I moved quietly closer on an intersecting path. As the deer approached, horror filled me. The newborn innocent had been hit by the tractor. It paused on the road, looking for its mother, and ran into the woods with its leg broken and bleeding. I tried to follow but couldn't keep up with it.

Feeling terrible about the doe, I returned to the Institute for help. They sent an expert tracker to find her. I lay down to rest and to meditate, but I couldn't get the doe out of my mind. Remember, I had broken my own leg years earlier and knew what it felt like.

I then decided to face a fearful old enemy of mine—pain. I went into deep meditation and made pain the focus with my full consciousness. I let myself feel my own pain. Opening wider, I felt the pain of my family, friends, and twenty years of clients. Feeling as if I would be crushed under the weight of all this pain yet somewhere realizing that I was surviving this experience, I willed myself to go into the nature of pain even more deeply and felt what seemed to be the pain of the whole world. Tears puddling in my ears and overflowing to soak the bed, mouth wide open to breathe under the annihilating weight, forcing myself defiantly to stay with the experience, with great rage I yelled out at the universe, "Why is there so much pain?"

Immediately I felt an indescribably powerful presence. It was filled with compassion and eclipsed my own sorrow at pain with its own. I got back an answer in an inaudible but strong and loving voice: "Freedom—Beauty." I gradually came out of my meditation, shaken but victorious. There was no feeling of being humbled by the presence; rather, it conveyed a great empowering respect for humans, including me.

I could buy the answer that I had received to my question about pain. It was the first answer that made sense to me. If God grants us freedom, we are allowed to drive tired and have an accident, or allowed to let our hate build until it is discharged against someone else. We are either free or we are not. Even God cannot create a square circle. Freedom is freedom. And it results in great pain as well as pleasure.

The beauty part also made sense. For there to be the magnificent abundance of resplendent diversity on this planet, everything has to eat something else and push against everything else for living space. Pain thus is intrinsic to both freedom and beauty. God, therefore, has to allow pain for both freedom and beauty to flourish.

Still, a compassionate intelligence could not bear this without there being a greater reality, a context in the infinity of time, or free of time, where a full peace and a dynamic harmony exists. It had always seemed to me that it was inelegant and insufficient that these two realities (one pain-filled and the other blissful) proceed one after another like acts in a play—Earth and then Heaven. For me the blissful reality has to be the greater eternal reality that is always present and always available to be perceived. In some way, physical matter and its suffering has to be as a dream in relation to fully awake, pure consciousness.

It is fine in dreams or in play to pretend to kill or be killed. In some way this physical existence is just a very serious game of pretend, through which consciousness can learn things that there is no other way to learn. Hence we live to learn about limits, and then die to remember our true nature.

The possibility may exist that we can remember while still immersed in physical reality—as in lucid dreaming,[29] where the dreamer wakes up enough to know that he is dreaming but remains asleep enough to continue the dream. God is always aware that this physical life is just a dream or a play. We can seek to be aware as well.

I am reminded of the time I went to my daughter's first play. She was in kindergarten. Her wise old teacher set up a simple play, *The Pied Piper of Hamlin*. The most advanced child got to be the piper. The other children got to be mice. All they had to do was follow the piper around and go "Squeak, squeak." What could go wrong?

A pounding scrambling could be heard behind the curtain, echoing through the silent cinderblock auditorium. The lights dimmed and the curtain rose, revealing twenty mice-children, staring straight ahead as if they were about to be shot. The kids were dead serious about how they looked and nervous they would forget their lines. As the play proceeded, bedlam began. Mice ran into each other from all directions, whiskers and tails akimbo. The young actors looked surprised, offended, and distressed yet proceeded through the play as each defined it. The play met all definitions of disaster.

The audience, however, comprised of parents, was overwhelmed with love and delight at their children's efforts. Tears of pride and love glistened on the faces of these moms and dads. Crying too, I thought, "This is how God must look at us in our struggles and errors." This play was perfect imperfection. If we could always look at ourselves with a love as pure as these parents had for their children, we would always feel safe and valued.

The preface of *A Course in Miracles* states: "Nothing real can be threatened. Nothing unreal exists. Herein lies the peace of God." I hope and feel that the deepest level of truth about reality is that this Earth existence is child's play, overseen by a loving God who invites us to awaken to the perfect imperfection of it all.

Something within Pete's death catalyzed my ability to finally sever the indoctrination of my parents, culture, religion, and twenty-two years of schooling. There was plenty of wisdom within all the information society had imparted to me, and I am grateful for all the love and energy that went into this education. It formed a platform from which to look far and wide. Yet, to fully live my life, I had to think for myself. My thinking coalesced into my philosophy—what is true for me. I choose to believe it until strong data to the contrary appears. In some ways I don't care whether my version of reality is truer than anyone else's. I simply need a positive and constructive model, in order for me to even want to go on with the game.

My model is that at the deepest level of reality there exists a completeness and a perfection. From this model, an image emerged that saved me from bitterness and fear. The image came in that second winter after Pete's death, while I was struggling with my own hardness and broken heart.

The image was of water. That liquid was the answer to my dilemma about openness and protection. If I viewed my heart, my feeling center, as a container filled with water—always complete in itself, yielding easily, full alone, full when embracing some object, full again when the object was removed—if I could do this, then I would indeed be open and nonresisting, yet unable to be devastated by the leaving of a love. I would still be full and complete whether I was embracing my beloved or separated from my beloved.

Again, myths are powerful influences on our perception and experience. Our myth of a broken heart, while speaking accurately of our pain, may do a great disservice to our true nature and underestimate the resilience of the human spirit. My myth of a water-like heart—strong and complete, yet yielding and embracing—reflects our ever-renewing nature.

I have had a chance to live my myth for a while now. Immediately after discovering my water image, I became more open, welcoming, and responsive toward people. Instantly my fear of hurt and feelings of lack decreased. And when my wife's grandmother, a women I dearly loved, died, there was some sadness but little pain. I seemed to be able to see beyond the drama of loss and see the beauty of her life and death. I could appreciate the beauty and dignity of myself and the loved ones around me, be fully involved in her dying, and yet at peace, even celebrating the process that was unfolding.

I can sense much more easily now when I shut down and go back to some fear form. I think I am beginning to learn the art of lucid-dreaming the dream we call life. My best indication that I am on the right path, for now, is the abundance of energy and love that I feel even when sad things happen—part of me being fully compassionate, part of me fully sorrowful, but a core within me singing sweet celebration and gratitude at the perfect imperfection of it all.

By now I have connected with Pete in several of my own meditations. My sense also is that he is now playful, lighthearted, friendly, and loving.

I have heard that in certain tribes, when a woman wants to

have a child, she quiets herself and listens carefully until she hears the song of her child. She mates and when first aware that she is pregnant, teaches the unborn child's song to the whole village. Her husband and everyone else in her life then sing the song during her pregnancy and at the birth of her child. They continue to sing the song to the infant, baby, and child as that child grows. It is sung then at important transitions, such as marriage, and finally at death of the body.

I think I have found my song. It is a song of deep joy and hope. I trust that my brother, freed now from all his distractions and drama, is singing his own eternal song. I have written this book from my heart to your heart. I hope that you, who have shared my journey through grief, find your own beautiful song that will sustain you through your own dark woundings and bright victories. Thank you for listening to mine.

RESOLUTION
February 14, 1993

Another year has passed.
Steel will worked too well.

I fear becoming untouchable
In my desire not to be hurt.

So I change once again
First searching a way.

Must we balance protection and pain?
I find my answer, praying.

No more bleeding images
Of hearts broken and torn.

Make your heart just like water
From which springs all life.

Whoever enters water is fully enveloped,
Surrounded, supported, sustained.

Whoever leaves water, leaves clean.
Water yields fully, losing only a drop.

And returns to completeness
Smooth, even, and full.

My heart is like water now
Full, and ready to receive.

My heart is like water now
Smooth, if you take leave.

I now can go lightly
Filled with joy and delight

Through funerals and partings
Which before gave me fright

And I am eager to meet you
With my warm water-like heart

Open to know you
Surrounding within.

Love lightens all
Love can begin.

Appendix ∞ P A M H O G A N
O N C H A N N E L I N G

In March of 1995 Pam Hogan graciously agreed to a phone interview about how she got started as a channel and what the experience has been like for her. What follows are edited excerpts from this conversation.

How did you get started channeling?

That is a bit of a story. The important pieces are this: In August of 1983 I was spending a lot of time walking in the woods close to my home. It was beautiful there, and I realized that when I walked I always watched my feet. I looked up one day and I started to cry about how beautiful the August woods were and the thought that came to me was that if I could appreciate beauty on that deep level then maybe I was beautiful too. Immediately a voice or a thought came to mind and showed me how it was all one—that we are all beautiful and of one energy.

At that moment, from the depths of my heart, I asked that everything that I touch from that moment forward be left in love. And that if I could speak with a high spiritual guide, I would share the teachings. This erupted from my heart at that moment and then I forgot about it.

In March of the next year I started receiving communications from ARGO. A loving voice, a strong mental imprint spoke to me, directing me on my spiritual path. Through many communications, many times . . . it is almost like many visits, a relationship developed with ARGO. When I asked ARGO why he came, he said, "Why dear child, because you asked." I could not remember asking at first. Then I thought back and I remembered that time in the woods.

A couple of years later I was looking in a book on Ascended Masters' instruction and it stated that a Master will seek out his student and that initiates first must ask from their hearts that everything they touch in life be left in love. And so, not knowing it at that time, I was opening up to being a student of a Master.

All of this has been confirmed though the years. It is a process, like any relationship, of developing trust, love, working together, and growing together. So what ARGO and I have is a relationship that is really a partnership, as he explains it, with my higher self and ARGO.

The letters ARGO stand for Ascended Rays of God's Oneness. ARGO is a conglomerate. It is a very elevated group of Master consciousness. So this is a group of higher consciousness that communicates through my Higher Self. So I am the physical piece.

Some within this ARGO group have lived on Earth. Some have not. There are Master teachers in this group. When I see ARGO, it is an energy of love. The blending of that consciousness is a cosmic being who is ARGO that I relate to specifically as a guide. ARGO is an androgenous being, a wonderful blend of the masculine and the feminine who exists as the composite of that thought-form of love and stands as gate-keeper for me. ARGO works with me, with my clearing out my own personal issues, so I can heal in my own life and be a clearer channel in love, for them.

Have some of your past-life existences been within ARGO?
They have suggested that I have connected with them before but not in a physical life.

It is beautiful energy!
It is wonderful energy and they show me now as the extension of it in the physical dimension.

Now, I have seen channelers as they channel. At the beginning of sessions, their faces distort and they often talk in an

accent of some sort. Did you go through a phase like that? Or was it more that the whispered voice would be there and you just say what the voice is telling you?

It was more like the whispered voice. But more than this, it is a very strong mental imprint. When ARGO first came, my face did not contort. I did not speak with an accent. I was aware in the beginning of really allowing energy to come fully through me, so that I could lose myself, and they could create. I could allow hand motion which you would see typical of a channel, you know, some of the hand positions. When they would first come, my face would grimace for a moment and then go into a very peaceful state. That happened initially but there was nothing of an accent.

And you would be conscious of what was being said?

Very much so.

When you say conscious channel, that is what you mean?

Yes. I am awake. And I have said to them, "You know, I trust you so much that I volunteer to be removed."

Their answer was beautiful. They said, "No, dear child, you believe that if you were present, God's message would not be, and we have come to teach you of your own God-source. And so it will be a partnership between your higher self and us."

Because of that, I have been able to learn as I channel. I have to grow and expand in order to maintain the channel. I am not being used. I am expanded while they are expanding their words through the physical world. It is a gift to me. It is in no way a taking from me or a use of me. I am a volunteer. And they are very clear that I am not in any way to allow myself to become victim of channeling. As a matter of fact, there are times when I have become really exhausted or overwhelmed. There was one point where they even threatened to leave because I was constantly going out and trying to help everybody. It never stopped. That was hurting me. And they would just not cooperate with anything that would damage me.

And it would hurt just because of a lack of balance in your life?

Well, energetically it takes quite a bit, so I was exhausted and I was finding that, no matter what the social situation, there was somebody that needed something and so I never had time off. It wasn't balanced. You know that it is all electromagnetic energy and ARGO exists at a greater vibration. In order to be able to hold that, you have to open to that level of energy. You are holding an unusual amount of electromagnetic energy. It can burn your rods. So you have to get clear and clearer—you know, the body, care of the emotional state, the mind, getting enough rest, balancing with play, having love in your life. All of those things raise your vibration.

Now, as I got to know ARGO, our energies blended more. At this point I can just put my head down and look of to the left a bit and just tell you what he is saying. There is none of the show of channeling in the sense there is no squeezed face even for a moment. Normally, what I will do is close my eyes so that I will stay very focused and not get distracted. Then I can feel their energy enter. But we are more in sync now, so the communication is much easier. And I have also learned, you know, how to balance myself in my life.

ARGO's presence is so powerful. At first I asked that no one tell anyone, thinking that it would ruin my business. I just started reading for a couple of my friends and word spread so quickly that I soon had to choose between doing this professionally and doing my old work. I chose this because of obvious reasons, because of the dimension of expansion for everyone as well as for myself. This was the way to go and I have never regretted it.

Almost immediately, as a matter of fact, within three months, there was a color photo of me and an article about me in the Sunday paper. I was on television. ARGO is just that powerful. So I was public almost right away. There was a lot of work in balancing that and being comfortable with suddenly being public.

You know that I was trained in social work. When I look

back at my life, I have been trained, I have been set up for this. Yes, that is the blend. I had started a business working with people with smoking cessation and weight control and I was doing one-on-one counseling out of my office, in Centerville, Ohio. That office then, of course, turned into my office for ARGO. So I was already set up in an office, it was all laid out for me. I just had to choose it.

And so at the beginning you did quite a bit in person. And now you do a majority of it by phone?

Now, because I have moved, I do a majority by phone. And also I have never advertised. It has always been word-of-mouth. The word spread to the East Coast and the Midwest, and even to Europe.

How far in training did you go in social work?

Just a B.A. I had applied to graduate school to pursue a masters in counseling but duties as a mother and life changes interfered with more schooling.

Did you have a fairly traditional Christian background?

Yes. I was raised Catholic and went to Catholic girls' schools even at the college level. Very much a traditional background although I had moved away from Catholicism for quite a while. I had done that toward the end of high school; although I studied at a Catholic college, I was removing myself rapidly from the religious philosophy and the ritual.

But you weren't real "New Age" when this started?

No. My husband David, who is now dead, was sick in the hospital. Suddenly, without understanding why, I began to move my hands over him to heal him. I asked him to visualize healing light moving through him at the same time. As we continued this process, his blood count, which was dangerously low, started to improve. Impressed by his progress, the physicians encouraged me to continue. At one point while David and I were working together a minister walked in on us. He understood hands-on healing and directed me to a book, *Argartha*. He also gave me the name of a man in town who was starting a study group around these teachings. I read the book, which I found very informative and comforting, and joined the group.

For one year I met with them on a weekly basis and fundamentally listened and observed. The group members were respected persons in the community. They would discuss the fundamental principles of Argatha's teaching and apply them to their lives. I spent my time absorbing this new consciousness, changing my old perceptions of God and the purposes of life. After a year of this study, ARGO contacted me. What a surprise!

Interesting. With the Catholic background and then it happening to you directly, was there much need to say, "Well is this real?"

Well. I questioned it, of course. So much of what ARGO has taught me in this past eight years just flew directly in the face of my traditional thoughts and my upbringing. Yet when I trusted . . . because I trusted what I felt and I moved with this, flying in the face of all my upbringing, it brought me to a greater state of consciousness and peace, although through turmoil in the meantime. That's what takes courage.

Have you come across anything that would be helpful for the general public to better understand channeling?

Well, I think like with everything, you have to be very careful in who you are talking with as a channel, you know the way you would chose a doctor or a psychiatrist. I asked ARGO the question specifically, and his response was you can trust channeling when you can see a change in consciousness— when you feel a change in your consciousness and your life experiences support that change in consciousness. It is the inner shift, and this is that peaceful connected place to God's Source. This is coming to your spiritual power. This is knowing your divine self. And your life experiences are going to come to you to support connection.

Many people, I believe, mistakenly believe, "I'll go to a

channel and then things will turn out the way I want them to. I am going to go to you so you will fix my life." And what a clear channel will do is work with the consciousness so the life adjusts around it. But there are times when what we would call a tragedy comes into your life so that you will expand your awareness. And that is not a negative although we tend to judge it as that. So that was what ARGO answered as to how would you know whether to trust a channel. How has your connection with this channel affected your state of consciousness? Where is your heart? Anyone who comes through my office or calls me, I warn them, "Run this all through your own filter and make your own decisions."

Now, there are spiritual pests that you hear about in the Bible. Someone who is psychic can make a connection with a disembodied spirit that is not necessarily of light that can also give correct information about something. I think this is where channeling gets a bad name. You have to look to the message. Is that channel turning you to your own power, is that channel working on embracing your heart—bringing you to a point of true self-awareness and talking to you about God's source?

If you are with a channel who is bossy, is telling you what to do, or is not really directing your soul but just giving you general information, you are probably with somebody who may be very well-intended but connected with another part of their consciousness that may hold some truth and may have something valuable to say but it may not be all the way connected with the highest spiritual teachers you want.

Sort of the old Ouija board, where you contact an entity that gets its kicks out of drawing some energy from the physical?

That can happen with the Ouija board where you throw the energies wide open—something powerful and wonderful can come through or something that is the shadow of that. You are open. So either can come through. There can be an imprint of the energy, let's say, of someone who has died or a famous person—and a playful spirit can get into the imprint and come and say I'm Abraham Lincoln and you were me in a past life and have a great time playing with you. So, that is the thing about the Ouija board. It is not innately good or evil but that is something of which you have to be very careful. If people are using one, they need to white light it and be very careful that they are not with anyone who is holding a lot of negativity or fear to attract those kinds of energy.

One of the things I had to work with ARGO is clearing the channel because it comes down . . . I always see it literally as a channel, as a column of light, and if some of my ego fears are in there the message may be misinterpreted. So the channel owes it to the people she is sharing the message with to continue to do her personal work. You would want to be with someone that you know is doing that, someone with a higher mind. You know, there may be a disaster coming, but if someone is using scare tactics you obviously don't want to be around her. If someone is looking and saying, Well, something unpleasant is happening but here is the higher viewpoint, stick with that counselor.

What was your pre-channel personality?

I think I tended to be rather skeptical. I was leading a pretty ordinary life. You know, I was very involved with my children and my family. Now a year after my husband David and I divorced, I was very stressed and saddened but nothing out of the ordinary. It was at that point I began walking in the woods. Certainly it was one of the lower points of my life. When I started to channel, I went to several therapists to get their impressions. Some said that I was the healthiest person they knew. None felt that I was mentally ill. They accepted the phenomenon of channeling in my life and supported me. They helped me cope with the changes occurring in my life.

So it sounds like you would describe yourself as emotionally balanced and level before this came along?

I guess as much as anybody. I wasn't hysterical. I would say that I am an emotionally based person, but I tended to run everything through my logic—screen it pretty carefully.

Why does ARGO come to help?

Their purpose really is to help everyone find God's source. I think that is very important statement to make. They don't come to fix our lives. They come to get us connected to our divine source. Our lives then start to reflect the connection. They have come to help. And apparently what I did was volunteer as a channel.

You have used in my channelings, as well as now, the term "God's source." Could you define it?

The divine spark, which can be termed also the creative spark, the God in all of us. This is the energy that we want to manifest through the physical dimension. It is love.

Thanks, Pam, for sharing all this personal information.

Sure. Hope it is helpful.

Notes

1. Robert Monroe, *Journeys Out of the Body* (New York: Doubleday, 1971).

2. Robert Monroe, *Far Journeys* (New York: Doubleday, 1985).

3. Franz Bardon, *Initiation into Hermetics* (Wuppertal, Germany: Deiter Ruggeberg, 1976).

4. Thomas Budzynski, *Clinical Applications of Non-Drug-Induced States*. In B.B. Wolman and M. Ullman (eds), *Handbook of States of Consciousness* (New York: Van Nostrand Reinhold Co., 1986).

5. Recent scientific studies are establishing with certaintude that these meditative states do exist and are dramatically different from normal waking consciousness in their neurophysiology and in how they are experienced. These meditative states can be monitored by using an electroencephalograph or EEG to find their associated brain-wave patterns. Also, current controlled studies confirm that the binaural beat sound patterns used by The Monroe Institute and others do actually change brain waves in a predictable way in the willing listener, more powerfully than placebos such as relaxing music. So we now have a technology that can aid a person in achieving states formerly obtained only through drugs or years of meditation practice. Michael Hutchison's book *Megabrain* provides a good overview of the consciousness technologies that now exist.

6. Bob Ortega, "Some Skeptics Become Believers After They Spend A Week Learning How To Get Out Of Their Bodies," *Wall Street Journal,* September 20, 1994.

7. Murray Cox, "Notes from the New Land," *Omni,* Vol 16, No. 1 (October 1993).

8. Gari Carter, *Healing Myself: A Hero's Primer for Recovery From Tragedy* (Charlottesville, VA: Hampton Roads Publishing Company, 1993).

9. Joseph McMoneagle, *Mind Trek* (Charlottesville, VA: Hampton Roads Publishing Company, 1994).

10. Ken Eagle Feather, *Traveling with Power: The Exploration and Development of Perception* (Charlottesville, VA: Hampton Roads Publishing Company, 1992).

11. Guidelines uses reverse engineering (taking the brain-wave patterns of talented subjects and using them to create new Hemi-Sync signals) to enhance the meditator's access to his Higher Self, and also to assist the meditator in experiencing out-of-body consciousness.

12. Robert Jahn and Brenda Dunne, "On the Quantum Mechanics of Consciousness, with Application to Anomalous Phenomena," *Foundations of Physics*, Vol 16, No 8 (August 1986); and Dean Radin and Roger Nelson, "Evidence for Consciousness-Related Anomalies in Random Physical Systems," *Foundations of Physics*, Vol 19, No 12 (December 1989).

13. Charles Tart, Ph.D., "Compassion, Science and Consciousness Survival," *Noetic Sciences Review*, Spring 1994.

14. Ronald Russell, ed., *Using the Whole Brain: Integrating the Right and Left Brain with Hemi-Sync Sound Patterns* (Charlottesville, VA: Hampton Roads Publishing Company, 1993).

15. Jane Roberts, *Seth Speaks* (New York: Bantam Books, 1974).

16. Pat Rodegast, *Emmanual's Book* (New York: Bantam Books, 1987) and *Emmanual's Book II* (Bantam Books, 1989).

17. Jose Stevens, Ph.D., and Simon Warwick-Smith, *The Michael Handbook: A Channeled System for Self-Understanding* (Orinda, CA: Warwich Press, 1988).

18. *A Course in Miracles* (Tiburon, CA: Foundation for Inner Peace, 1985).

19. The phrase "My body carries me for nothing" is paraphrased from "Finding the Father" by Robert Bly in *Iron John* (New York: Addison-Wesley Publishing Company, 1990), p. 21.

20. At the time of the final re-write of this book, on January 26, 1996, we had to euthanize our Border collie. It was a tough decision brought about by extreme diabetes. My daughter, now eleven years old, witnessed the event and helped dig the grave, placing three heart-shaped objects on top, symbolizing our love for a dear and loyal pet. As we cried together it was clear that it was healthy grief for a good dog who had enjoyed a good life. Blackie was a champion Frisbee catcher. If you laid down a luscious steak and threw a Frisbee at the same time, she would go after the Frisbee. As we finished the funeral, my daughter specifically requested I add this footnote to my book, in remembrance of Blackie. I am happy to do so. I miss Blackie too.

21. David Feinstein and Peg Elliott Mayo, *Rituals for Living and Dying* (San Francisco: HarperSanFrancisco, 1990).

22. Brain L. Weiss, M.D., *Many Lives, Many Masters* (New York: Simon and Schuster Inc., 1988).

23. Raymond Moody, Jr., M.D. *Life After Life* (New York: Bantam, 1975) and *Coming Back* (New York: Bantam, 1991).

24. The many books on the subject include: Melvin Morse, M.D., with Paul Perry, *Closer to the Light* (New York: Villard Books, 1990); Melvin Morse, M.D., with Paul Perry, *Transformed by the Light* (New York: Villard Books, 1992); Betty J. Eadie, *Embraced by the Light* (Placerville, CA: Gold Leaf Press, 1992).

25. E.J. Gold, *American Book of the Dead* (San Francisco, HarperSanFrancisco, 1995).

26. Michael Newton, Ph.D., *Journey of Souls* (St. Paul, MN: Llewllyn Publications, 1994).

27. Neale Donald Walsch, *Conversations with God: an Uncommon Dialogue* (Charlottesville, VA: Hampton Roads Publishing Company, 1995).

28. Robert Monroe, *Ultimate Journey* (New York: Doubleday, 1994).

29. Lucid Dreaming is the art of becoming conscious during dream sleep and then being able to take control of the content of the dream. Steven LaBerge is an acknowledged authority on this phenomenon and has developed a device designed to signal sleepers when they have entered a dream.

You may contact the Monroe Institute for more information about its research, tapes, and programs at the following address:
The Monroe Institute
Route 1 Box 175
Faber, VA 22938-9749
(804) 361-1252
Fax ((804) 361-1237
E-Mail: MonroeInst@AOL.com

You may contact Pam Hogan at the following address:
Pam Hogan
P.O. Box 7041
Taos, NM 87571
(505) 751-3839

The author, Joseph Gallenberger, is interested in your reactions to his book. He is available for workshops and presentations. He can be contacted through Hampton Roads Publishing Company, via phone, letter, or E-mail.

BOOKS OF RELATED INTEREST

MY LIFE AFTER DYING
George G. Ritchie, Jr. M.D.
Introduction by Ian Stevenson, M.D.

"George Ritchie's story of his dying and coming back to life after some magnificent spiritual experiences is worth reading by all those who have any concern in the 'beyond.' To know that he was the inspiration that started Raymond Moody on his series of investigations into the afterlife makes him noteworthy." — **Spiritual Frontier**

5½ x 8½ trade paper, 170 pages, ISBN 1-878901-25-7, $9.95

HEALING FEELINGS, THOUGHTS AND MEMORIES
Serene West

Here are practical techniques for dealing with specific problems, such as anger, grief, worry, criticism, and fear, and a 30-day "spiritual vitamin" supply which provides affirmations and meditations for common problems in life such as making right choices, finding love, gaining self-confidence, and many others.

5¼ x 8¼ trade paper, 136 pages, ISBN 1-878901-09-5, $8.95

PAST LIVES, FUTURE GROWTH
Armand Marcotte and Ann Druffel

Psychic Armand Marcotte helps people with their problems, ranging from incest, suicide, and violent crimes to problems of marriage and divorce. Interestingly, he frequently finds that people's problems are rooted in previous lifetimes. *Past Lives, Future Growth* tells some of these stories.

5½ x 8½ trade paper, 216 pages, ISBN 1-878901-79-6, $8.95

PHANTOMS AFOOT: *Helping the Spirits Among Us*
Mary Summer Rain

Mary Summer Rain's Indian teacher showed her how to use the power and follow the path of a dreamwalker. Under her guidance, Mary confronts wayward spirits who inhabit a timeless dimension between spiritual planes and helps them move on to other realities. In the process she learns of our spiritual obligation to all life.

5½ x 8½ trade paper, 336 pages, ISBN 1-878901-64-8, $12.95

USING THE WHOLE BRAIN
Ronald Russell, Editor

Tens of thousands of people have used The Monroe Institute's Hemi-Sync technology to gain new control over their lives. *Using the Whole Brain* is the first book to tell what it can do for body, mind, and spirit. Everything from coping with surgery to strengthening concentration to facilitating transcendent events such as out-of-body experiences and remote viewing. Preface by Robert Monroe.

5½ x 8½ trade paper, 264 pages, ISBN 1-878901-86-9, $14.95

SOULMAKER
Michael Grosso, Ph.D.
Foreword by Whitley Strieber

"*'Experiences are soulmaking, if they shatter our routine image of self or soul, if they undo our fixed ideas of who and what we are...' writes the author. The book reads like a diary of such encounters, not just his but many others as well. Grosso is convinced that we are in the midst of an 'epidemic of impossible experiences' that foreshadows a revolution of consciousness.*" — *NAPRA ReVIEW*

5½ x 8½ trade paper, 160 pages, ISBN 1-878901-21-4, $9.95

MAGIC AND LOSS
Greg Raver Lampman

"*My own confrontation with mortality stunned me, coming when it seemed I was far too young. . . . I learned that I suffer from an illness that, almost certainly, will be terminal.... The letters compiled here...were my private communications, my legacy to my [three-year-old] daughter, my recording of my love for her.*"

Magic and Loss takes the reader through a full range of emotions: shock, grief, anger, depression, to joy and an appreciation of the sacred now.

"*Heroic and touching . . .*" — *Reader's Digest*

5½ x 8½ cloth, 184 pages, ISBN 1-57174-017-1, $18.95
5½ x 8½ trade paper, 184 pages, ISBN 1-57174-015-5, $9.95

Hampton Roads Publishing Company
publishes books on a variety of subjects,
including metaphysics, health, alternative medicine,
visionary fiction, and other related topics.
For a copy of our latest catalog, call toll-free,
(800) 766-8009, or send your name and address to:

Hampton Roads Publishing Company, Inc.
134 Burgess Lane
Charlottesville, VA 22902